D0594994

FALSE SECURITY

*Has the New Age Given
Us a False Hope?*

False Security

*Has the New Age Given
Us a False Hope?*

BY JERRY PARKS

HUNTINGTON HOUSE PUBLISHERS

Copyright © 1993 by Jerry Parks
All rights reserved. No part of this book
may be reproduced without permission from the
publisher, except by a reviewer who may quote brief
passages in a review; nor may any part of this book
be reproduced, stored in a retrieval system, or
copied by mechanical, photocopying, recording
or other means, without permission
from the publisher.

Huntington House Publishers
P. O. Box 53788
Lafayette, Louisiana 70505

ISBN 1-56384-012-X
Library of Congress Card Catalog Number
92-73708

Contents

Introduction

Twenty years ago the Lord began dealing with me on the condition of my life and the truths contained in His Word. At that time I was living in an area just outside our nation's capital. Because my job involved travel, I spent much time stuck in traffic jams on the capital beltway and touring the busy streets of Washington D.C. I found that my time was increasingly becoming occupied with Christian radio. Now, I had been raised in a fundamentalist, evangelical environment by my Christian parents, but it wasn't until this time in my life that the Holy Spirit's impact began to produce spiritual fruit. Oh, I had come to believe in the Lord. I knew that He was real, but no matter how hard I tried, I could never please Him. In my own mind—I just wasn't good enough for a Holy God. I was a head-knowledge-believer without a new heart—thus no assurance of salvation from the fires of Hell. But God had plans to change all that!

It was during those times, riding in a car, listening to Christian radio, that my hunger increased for God's Word. The Lord actually used two vehicles to influence me. The first, as I already mentioned was Christian radio. The other was "The Cross and the Switchblade," by David Wilkerson. David, as you know, was the founder of Teen Challenge in New York City. One of the ministry's branches is located in Rehrersburg, Pennsylvania. This ministry had touched some very dear friends of ours, Dick and Carol Davidson, who lived close to Rehrersburg just outside of Hershey. It was Dick and Carol who had given us Dave Wilkerson's book.

God in His wisdom had set the stage for the impact that David's book was to have in my life by drawing me into His Word. This was done through the radio programs that I had been hearing. The program that had the greatest influence on my life was the "Jewish Voice Broadcast" out of Phoenix, Arizona. The testimonies heard on these daily programs had created in me a hunger for God's Word, unlike anything I had ever experienced before. Jews were being saved and coming to the Messiah. Their lives were being miraculously changed, and I was growing more and more hungry for a touch from this same Redeemer. A touch that would bring about change from the hypocrisy that I had been living!

During this time I would come home from work and sit and read the Bible for hours at a time. And, I might add that God was blessing those days. There were times that tears would be running down my face to the point that I would be concerned that Ellen or the kids might see me and not understand. I firmly believe that during those days the Lord was making me clean through His word (John 15:3). You see, I was beginning to see Jesus, and to recognize that only He could do for me what my heart longed for. I wanted a freshness and cleanness; and a usefulness and peace which could only come from a personal touch and an ongoing relationship with the Lord. Because of what I had been hearing, I knew that this must be possible as I was seeing what God intended through the Scriptures, as well as hearing it first-hand through the "Jewish Voice."

During those days God did three things for me. First, He gave me a longing to see Him face to face. This is a longing that I still possess—or should I say that still possesses me! Secondly, He gave me a love, a deep love for the Jews, a love which was unnatural as I discovered later. But, this was genuine—this was God loving through me—it was a love that wanted to sacrifice for the Jew! This too, is still a burning desire of my heart, and though I have had many occasions to witness to the Jews, whom I've worked with—yet, that love still drives me, for the nation remains unsaved. And there was a third thing that was happening—God was blessing my search. The more that I longed for Him the more I longed for His word and for the fellowship of His people. And God who is faithful was also drawing my darling wife, Ellen, to Himself, but in a totally different way.

Now that I was ripe for it—*The Cross and the Switchblade* was about to play a lasting role in my life. While reading it alone one night in our home, I was filled for the first time with the Holy Spirit. Salvation was no longer a vague concept—it was now a reality! David Wilkerson's life was showing me what true commitment of one's life to the Lord meant; and as I saw the dedication of his life to the Lord—I began to see that God alone could do for me what all along I had been trying to do for myself. For you see, I had been trying to make myself good enough for God to accept, and I could not achieve that level of righteousness—no matter what I did, or how hard I tried. God only wanted from me a willing committed life, and that night I presented myself to Him—accepting what my Lord and Savior had done for me on the cross two thousand years before. He wanted to be not only my Savior but my Lord. That night He became both Lord and Savior! I now knew that it was no longer my works, but it was the Lord's work through me that counted.

I was now able to understand just how privileged I was. My heritage was increased; my family was expanded. Now, it shouldn't be hard to understand that my love for the Jews was naturally accompanied by a strong desire to see them saved. After all it was their rejection that made it possible for my adoption into God's family. This desire to see them saved led me to search the Scriptures for clues to their salvation. This search naturally led to a study of the kingdom and the end of the age.

God has promised that we will know the truth. I believe that over the years understanding has come forth from the pages of Scripture revealing God's plan for the Jew and the end of the age. This book is meant to be an aid to your understanding of the end times. Some might ask why God would choose an ordinary layman to write such a book. Believe me, I have asked that question on several occasions myself. However, no one seems to be challenging the thinking of God's people on the scriptural truths surrounding this subject. I believe that God's truth can be discerned from Scripture, and should not be confusing. If you have never read the Bible, you are going to be amazed at what God's Word teaches. If you have read the Bible, you are going to find that your own questions are similar to those that led me to embark on this study. You see, the Holy Spirit has been sent to the Church to lead us into all truth. You are going to find that truth, when put into the context of God's plan, will dissolve your most confounding questions.

Yet, there will be many who will pick up this book and begin to read who will, because of bondage to tradition or fear, put it down. WHY? Because this book will take the Word of God and the truths contained therein, and it will present them as a challenge to what you have been taught concerning the Second coming of our Lord. I encourage you to read the book and study the Bible on this subject, for in so doing you will be strengthened. IF THE WORDS OF THIS BOOK ARE CORRECT, GOD WILL REVEAL IT TO YOU. I believe the message to be true to God's Word. I believe that coming to understand God's plan will strengthen your own belief, which will add to your growth as a Christian. This book will, I believe, answer questions that you have had on this subject. God bless you as you read and study.

ONE

WHY ALL OF THE CONCERN?

In recent years we have seen the elimination of a bi-polar world, which coexisted in a state of cold war due to the threat of destruction. Today that has all changed and we hear much of a "new world order." Not only is the world undergoing major change, but this new order is also showing stamina through testing. Its first test was in the Middle East with Iraq, but the test that held just as much potential for world-wide chaos was the August 1991 coup within the Soviet Union. Under both of these tests the new order held. It not only held within the leadership of the world, but within the general populace itself. At least in the eyes of man we have genuine potential for world peace! The advance of democracy eastward is being seen as a significant achievement for the world as a whole. Yet, while democracy is advancing eastward, Eastern religious ideas are making their way rapidly into Western culture. The world is indeed close to being unified even as these words are being penned.

There remains at least one major challenge before peace can be brought to this world, and for that reason our attentions are even more focused on the Middle East. A resolution to the Arab-Israeli conflict is uppermost in the minds of world leaders. Men are working feverishly for just such a peace.

With these great changes actually occurring on the world scene, more and more people in the Church

13

are pointing to the return of the Lord Jesus. Yet, among theologians there is still uncertainty surrounding the timing of the Rapture as it relates to the Great Tribulation. Most are saying that we will escape this time of great fear and distress, which could at this moment be drawing very near. Others say that we may see the devastation. And then there are those within the Church who say that this potential for peace could actually be the beginning of the Millennium and the Lord's rule over the earth through the Church. No one has presented clear scriptural evidence to allow the Church in unified fashion to see God's plan.

As a result of what we are seeing and hearing in our day, there are many questions that beg for answers. First, we might ask, does God really want the Church to be disoriented as these times grow more tense, or would He want a unified Church in these confusing days? The answer would seem very clear—the Lord Jesus had prayed in John 17 for this unity. Is it then expecting too much for Christians to be in unity on the Second Coming? Does the Bible really leave us in darkness on this subject? The Bible itself says No! Listen: "But you are not in darkness, brethren, for that day to surprise you like a thief."[1] God's purpose for the Church must be understanding or light. Have the modern views on the timing of the rapture been able to give—us the assurance of this promised light? But, an even more perplexing question arises in light of today's events—just where will today's Church be when the much-talked-about peace through this new world order fails, and the Antichrist comes forth in wrath to persecute those "who keep the commandments of God and bear testimony to Jesus"?[2]

Our not knowing what will happen to the Church today or tomorrow is a situation which creates an environment of darkness, not light! The most popular view of the Rapture teaches the imminent return of our Lord. This return could take place before you finish reading this sentence, or it may not take place for hundreds of years. But we are told, "But you are not in darkness, brethren, for that day to surprise you like a thief." Ironically, this and most of the other Rapture views of our day leave the otherwise enlightened Church in darkness on this most important doctrine. We must conclude that either the Bible does have clear teaching on this subject, and we just have not listened to it; or that this verse has misled us, and we are not in the light at all, but in darkness. Now, since God is true, after much research I believe that the Bible does, in fact, have the clear answers concerning our Lord's coming. It has been estimated that somewhere in the neighborhood of 25% of Scripture speaks on this subject. Would it not then seem reasonable to think that our understanding is important to the Lord?

Dave Hunt, in his book *Global Peace and the Rise of Antichrist*, quotes Charles Spurgeon and his passionate view on truth: "May there ever be found some men ... who shall denounce again and again all league with error and all compromise with sin, and declare that these are the abhorrence of God ... The destruction of every sort of union which is not based on truth is a preliminary to ... the unity of the Spirit."[3]

Unfortunately, constructive criticism within the Church today is seen as promoting disunity. Yet, what Spurgeon was saying is that it is necessary to stand for truth and not compromise, and only then can true unity come about! Dave Hunt further stated: "If ever there was a time when we needed to ask God for wisdom and seek to understand what His Word has prophesied for our own day, this is that time."[4]

I believe in the leading and teaching of the Holy Spirit in the life of one who is seeking God's truth. I further believe that the Bible is the only basis for truth, and truth changes our entire perspective.

You might be asking why a book on the Second Coming would change one's outlook? Well, let me attempt to answer that with another question. If you knew for sure that the souls of many that you love would soon be in danger, possibly within the next one to fifteen years (now remember I said if you knew for sure), would that bring about change in your approach to your mission in life? Just thinking that it could be true has changed my own commitment! And if proven true, I'm certain that it would also cause you to attempt to increase your own commitment and the commitment of your loved ones. We certainly can't be sure of the one- to fifteen-year time frame, but we can know the times and seasons. And many are viewing the signs of our times and seeing them already ripe for prophetic fulfillment.

Do we have the mind of Christ on this matter?

You may be thinking, but my life is secure—I have no reason to change it. And to this I can only say PRAISE GOD!! But, I wonder if you've considered that today perhaps the greatest conspiracy of all times is under way to deceive and, if possible, destroy the very elect. The conspiracy of which I speak is Satan's plan. The events that we are seeing fulfilled on the world scene today are thought by many to be a fulfillment of prophecy, and thus are potentially a major part of this plan. Yet, the real question is just what part of Satan's plan have we (the church) bought into?

Let's consider what our Lord said in Matthew 24:4-28, in answer to His disciples' question concerning His coming. "Take heed that no one leads you astray. For many will come in my name, saying, 'I am the Christ,' and they will lead many astray." The Lord indicates to us that this will happen over time, for he says, "the end is not yet," but there's more. "Then," he says in verse 9, "they will deliver you up to tribulation." And He tells of those who would hate the disciples, and of the falling away of many. Then he calls for us to "endure." But who are those who will be present during the Tribulation? My contention is that *we* will be here during this time, and that *you* and *I* are those who the disciples represent.[5] My contention, however, is not what's important—it's the scriptural evidence that's important.

Have you ever wondered why the Lord placed this warning within Scripture? And have you wondered just why He would direct this message, according to many teachers of our day, only to the Jews of the nation Israel, those who are not yet saved? Have you wondered how the nation Israel could be seduced by false christs, so as to fall away from the faith, when in fact they'll not even be saved as a nation until the very end of the age? I pose these questions because most Bible teachers of our day, those who are Pre-tribulationalists, believe all of these facts as stated, and yet teach that this passage is meant for the nation Israel only, and that its purpose is to tell them when the Lord will return. Yet you and I and other Christians like us, down through the ages, are those who've seen these false christs. I'm confident that you'll see the problem with this teaching, as we search to answer these and other questions.

You see, as I began to be drawn into my own study of the Bible, one thing that I quickly came to understand was that there was much confusion on the subject of prophecy in our day.

It all started when someone gave me the book *The Late Great Planet Earth*. To me, the book was awe-inspiring, presenting Jesus as the only possible true and living Christ. But just as many radio preachers had done, the book left me with many unanswered questions concerning our Lord's return, and coupled with the controversies heard over radio, I embarked on what has now been an extended search for scriptural answers to these questions. I was looking for teaching that was supported by the Word of God. You see, the facts stated by Lindsay and others just were not adding up with what was occurring within the Jewish community in our own day. I could see God was doing a mighty work among the Jews. I was also seeing in Scripture that the Jews were the foundation of the Church. At Pentecost, approximately 50 days after the resurrection of our Lord, 3000 Jews were added to the Church. Also, there were twelve Jews who were called to be the apostles in the Church. The modern Jews, who were accepting Messiah in our day, were just like Jews of old. I was hearing testimonies of men and women who were dead as far as their families were concerned. Funerals were actually held by parents who were heart-broken by the loss of a child from their faith. Men and women were paying a great price for conversion, which the predominantly gentile Church today often takes for granted.

Yet Christianity, to which all races were committing their lives, was a Jewish religion. The Messiah (the Savior) was the promised Savior of the Jews, and we by grace were being allowed to be grafted in. It was God who spoke by the Old Testament prophets of the re-grafting of the Jews in the last days. It was God who had promised to them a new heart (a New Covenant). Yet, Lindsay and others were saying that the Jewish nation upon their conversion would not be a part of this Church that God was building. They would not be a part of the Bride of Christ. I had to know what was occurring! These men had not answered my questions. God had promised to save the Jews, and yet they wouldn't be a part of the Church. I had to reconcile this in my own mind. Was it possible that I was overlooking something in these events, and in the teaching of Matthew 24?

But discovering just to whom this passage in Matthew 24 is written wasn't the real reason for my concern. My reason was this: I believe that the days described in this passage are already upon us. Now, these are strong words, but consider these facts. The satanic plan, which has given rise to all of the false christs who've dared to come over the past 2000 years, has now in our day been brought forth in great power disguised by the angel of light himself. If you are like most Christians, you're asking: what is this satanic plan? If you are asking this, you're not alone, for there are enough books written on the subject to fill a major portion of any average library, yet most are unaware of "the plan." Now, these books aren't written by Christians, as one might suspect, but by believers in the plan itself.

Lack of unity in today's theology

As an introduction to this question, let us first take a look at the beliefs of our day concerning whether or not we will be here during the Great Tribulation, which many believe will arise out of the political and religious climate of our day.

Many of our leaders agree that the time of Antichrist is quickly approaching; yet most would differ on the subject of the Second Coming of the Lord. Most evangelicals and fundamentalists today believe that God has set up dispensations or ages marked by changes in the way God works in His creation. Unfortunately, even among dispensationalists there are differences in what determines an age. There are also several other views which are not dispensational, such as Covenant, the Reconstructionist, or the Reformed theologians. This may shock you, but I believe that none of these are completely correct. I believe that the more allegorical interpretations (amillennialism and post-millennialism) are incorrect. These are big terms confirming the confusion over the literal earthly reign of Christ. Although the Millennium is a subject of this book, it will not be our main focus.

The Scripture has always spoken literally and plainly on the subject of prophetic events. I believe that God has preserved the interpretation of prophetic Scriptures dealing with the end times for the people of those times. Just as He gave understanding of preserved scriptural truth to His people in the days just prior to the arrival of the Messiah (even though Israel's religious leaders had misunderstood the truths concerning the Lord's first coming), even so I believe that He will give understanding to those of the generation who will view the Second Coming. "Surely the Lord God will do nothing, but he revealeth his secret unto his servants the prophets" (Amos 3:7 KJV).

The Reformed theologian progresses on the right track, but makes a critical mistake. He sees the Christian alone as the heir to God's covenants, and therefore leaves the nation Israel completely out. He sees the Jews as a people rejected by God, due to their own blindness concerning the Messiah, who had been sent for them. Some other visionary thinkers have even carried this doctrine to its extreme by seeing the Western world akin to Britain as being those tribes of Israel who were lost (these are called British Israelites). Unfortunately, British Israelism also refuses to see God's promises to bless Israel . . . in both the Old and New Testaments as still being a reality. Instead, they lay claim to these promises, and see America as the Promised Land. Others such as Reconstructionists and Dominionists are preaching even more dangerous theories.

We dispensationalists have problems of our own. Many of us attempt to read entirely too much into Scripture that isn't really there. Most lay claim to a literal interpretation of Scripture, and yet proceed to allegorize, or disregard altogether, scriptures which don't fit the system. If you question them, they just simply write you off as unenlightened. They, in fact, overlook many of the literal alternatives in Scripture, and often substitute the literal meaning with their own theories.

Why should we reject much of the popular teaching concerning the Lord's Second Coming? And if we have rejected much, what is left? First, we must consider the reasons for rejection of established systems of end-time theology. The reason is simple. Many of the present day teachings are just not completely literal in their interpretation of prophetic scriptures. It is not that these teachings are totally erroneous, it's just that there is error within each system. If we're to consider that every prophecy concerning the first coming of Messiah was literally fulfilled to the letter, then we must expect every prophesy pointing to the Second Coming to be literal in its fulfillment. If this is true, then we must see Christ's return as being pre-millennial. We therefore must see Christ as coming back bodily to this earth to rule for 1000 years, as the scriptures clearly state. However, we still have a problem because each of the pre-millennial systems of theology (those who believe in the 1000 year reign) are rightly accused of having by-passed a literal interpretation of Scripture in some areas. And it is these changes in literal meaning which create a major difference in the meaning as it relates to prophecy.

Now, I realize that some of you don't believe that there will be an actual 1000-year reign of Christ on this earth, but your position is not adhering to the literal statements contained in Scripture. After all, considering all of the confusion, it's very possible that we are all

overlooking the truth on this subject. Taking God's
Word literally has challenged my own thinking.

Just to show that the amillennialists and the post-
millennialists are not the only ones confused, I want
you to consider the following statements by one of the
foremost pre-millennialists. Here are two statements,
both contained on the same page of Hal Lindsay's new
book, *The Road to Holocaust*: "The only major sign that
is not yet visible is the appearance of the Antichrist and
the False Prophet. But I do not believe they can be
manifested until the Church has been snatched out in
the Rapture." (After making this statement, Lindsay
then makes the following statement in the very next
paragraph.)

> This is a time when every Christian should be so
> thankful to God that He has revealed the future
> course of history to us. We are rapidly entering
> the most fearful period in human history. Only
> those who know and believe the prophetic Scrip-
> tures in a plain literal sense will be able to have
> the inner strength, peace, and stability in the days
> ahead to seize the opportunities to evangelize.
> They are the only ones also who will not be
> deceived by Satan's ultimate counterfeit, the
> Antichrist. He will bring in a plan for world
> political and religious unification which will re-
> sult in a pseudo-peace that will deceive many of
> the elect. And he will do this with the accomplish-
> ment of "signs, wonders and false prophecies."
> (Matt 24:11,24)[6]

How can Lindsay believe that we are gone, and
yet believe that we will be the ones not deceived by the
Antichrist? Perhaps Dr. Geisler in his book, *False Gods
of Our Times*, has said it better than I when he said in
his argument against the New Age, "A person can
persuade someone who desires to be rational and
noncontradictory against pantheism by showing him
the irrational and contradictory nature of panthe-

ism."[7] Certainly it is not just the New Age pantheist who needs to get his theology straightened out.

However, my concern for Bible truth is no less than Geisler's. When I look for literal interpretation, I'm looking for rational thought, for it's irrational to believe that God's Word is truth and yet to twist it, or to say that it means something entirely different than what it appears to be saying. But as pointed out, there is another side to the literal coin, and that is contradiction. If we allow contradictions to enter in, then what we teach becomes irrational to a rational mind. Yet, contradiction is exactly what we see in Lindsay's statements.

In order that you might see that Lindsay is not the only one making such contradictory statements, consider the following from Grant Jeffrey:

"Paul specifically warns us to be watchful, hopeful and joyful as we see the beginning signs of 'the last days' because it means the Rapture is close at hand."[8]

However, just two pages earlier in his book he writes:

> There are *no preconditions* to the Rapture. There are *no events* that must occur prior to Christ calling His Church home to heaven. In fact, if Christ had raptured the Church in the first century, the end-time events would still have occurred on schedule in this generation without contradicting a single prophecy about the final crisis for Israel in this generation.[9] (emphasis mine)

In Jeffrey's first statement we are to be watchful, hopeful, and joyful as we see these signs, then he says that there are no signs—"There are no preconditions." We can't have it both ways.

You see, my concern is this—if Christians can attack other religions which use the Scriptures for their doctrine (e.g., the Jehovah's Witnesses), attacking their doctrine based upon scriptural truth and rationality, then we must be free from confusion in our own doctrine. In other words, we have to make sense. The Scriptures say, "Come, let us reason together." Bible truth therefore must be understood by the rational mind once the blinders have been removed by the new birth.

The challenge that I had, therefore, in my own search for biblical truth was to look at all of the systems of theology which teach the return of the Lord prior to His 1000-year reign in an attempt to find the answers—answers which would allow a literal interpretation and still be consistent in clearing up the problems created within each of the present systems. Consideration had to be given to each of the following: the pre-trib, mid-trib, post-trib, and partial-rapture theories.

The covenants

In my attempt to clear up the confusion presented within the various teachings of Christianity on this subject, I knew that another critical issue existed, besides the Millennium, that had to be considered. This issue was the question of what to do with the people of the New Covenant (the Church and the nation Israel). My theory was that the people of this covenant can't be divided, if we are to interpret Scripture literally. They must be one. Paul had certainly taught that there is no longer Jew or gentile under the New Covenant. He also taught that the nation Israel will one day be saved under this same New Covenant by which you and I are saved. Yet those who believe in any rapture theory prior to the end of the Great Tribulation divide the people of the New Covenant. They attempt to place a saved Israel literally in their land at the end of this age without a resurrection body, and they attempt to place her there apart from the other people of the New Covenant (the Church). Now, we know that the New Covenant is obviously made with Israel, and in order for her to enter the kingdom age, Scripture teaches that she must also accept this New Covenant (please remember that this is the same New Covenant which the Church has accepted). The Word emphasizes the covenants as foundational to God's plan for mankind, yet they are the source of confusion.

You see, I operate from one basic premise when considering Scripture, and that is that God's truth is simple. It has to be simple in order for me, and others like me, to understand it. I find that the only reason that it is not simple is because man confuses it in its interpretation.

If we do not begin with right understanding, or else find it somewhere along the line, then we cannot possibly end right. And God provides One who will teach us and do it right if we'll let Him. This One is none other than His Holy Spirit. Therefore, if we're listening, He will set us on the right track. To properly understand prophecy, we must begin at the beginning.

I believe that the Holy Spirit took me to the foundation for all of prophecy when He allowed me to see that God's covenants are the basis for a proper understanding of prophecy. We who interpret Scripture literally seem to have no problem with the Abrahamic covenant. We know that it's the promise of land in the Middle East and dominion over that land. However, prophecy begins to take different paths with the understanding of this covenant, because it is not always taken literally. There are those who see it as being completely replaced by the New Covenant. Thus, to them, both it and the people of the covenant, the nation Israel, are done away with in God's plan. On the other hand, there are those who believe that the covenant must be fulfilled for Israel. I would fall into this group. Why? Because God made a promise to Abraham which was confirmed by many prophecies in later years. We also know that Abraham believed God, and that God will not break His promise. However, those who believe as I do, must ask—has the covenant been fulfilled? The answer obviously is—NO! For its fulfillment must be to the letter, otherwise, it's not literal. Therefore, I concluded that its fulfillment is still future, just as we dispensationalists have believed all along. I also realized that if we are to stick with a literal interpretation, then we can't spiritualize the fulfillment of the Abrahamic covenant as some do.

The same principle, of course, holds true for the Davidic covenant. It can be taken literally, with Christ as the heir to David's throne. If we expect the covenant to be literally fulfilled, then the Lord Jesus will rule during the Millennium as Scripture promises. He will rule as the physical heir to David's throne.

Although I could easily understand these promises and their literal fulfillment, the New Covenant seemingly clouded the issue (Jer. 31:31-34). Understanding the New Covenant is possibly the key to clearing up the confusion on prophecy. This covenant seems to be a spiritual covenant. Under it, men experience a spiritual new birth, and thus we see divisions again taking place in interpretation. Some have integrated the Old Covenants into this New Covenant, claiming the kingdom promises for the Church, and seeing it as a spiritual kingdom. Others have totally separated the two. Those who integrate the two covenants, spiritualize both, thus doing away with the need for a literal fulfillment of the earthly kingdom. Yet, those who spiritualize the New Covenant and retain a literal interpretation of the land Covenant (some dispensationalists), completely separate the two covenants, as well as the people of the two covenants (the Church and Israel). All of this can be confusing. No wonder so many say that we can't really know the answers here. The covenants seem to be the source of confusion. Yet, I found that to God they are the source of His plan.

But which understanding is correct? I believe that none of the popular teachings of our day are correct. The reason is this: they all ignore one very important point, that both the Old and the New Covenants were meant for the same people. In other words, Jesus came to die not only for the rebirth of the Jew and Gentile within the Church, but also for the rebirth of the nation Israel. Listen to what John's gospel says on this subject:

> So the chief priests and the Pharisees gathered the council, and said, "What are we going to do? For this man performs many signs. If we let him go on thus, every one will believe in him, and the Romans will come and destroy both our holy place and our nation." But one of them, Caiaphas, who was high priest that year, said to them, "You know nothing at all; you do not understand that it is expedient for you that one man should die for the people, and that the whole nation should not perish."

(John now adds the following comments concerning this prophecy):

> He did not say this of his own accord, but being high priest that year he prophesied that Jesus should die for the nation, and not for the nation only, *but to gather into one* the children of God who are scattered abroad. (John 11:47-52, emphasis mine)

The promise was to the Jew, the nation Israel, the children of Abraham, and John makes it clear that it is also for the Church. This fact could not be ignored. As I continued my search, theory turned into a premise based upon the facts discovered within Scripture. This premise was that both the land promise and the New Covenant promise to Israel must be integrated in the end for all of God's people. Therefore, all people of the New Covenant will become heirs of the old and reign with Christ, possessing the promised land. Thus, a literal integration of the three covenants will occur. In all of my study, I have not once seen a literal integration attempted by modern theologians. Yet this, after many years of study, is what I believe the literal teaching of Scripture is telling us. This premise was also supported by the fact that 17th-century puritan England strongly believed that one day the nation Israel would join the Church and produce great blessing for all. Our founding fathers came from these roots. Have we left the truths they taught? Is this the reason for the confusion? If you complete the reading of this book, you will see.

Dave Hunt had this to say concerning the covenants:

> Before the cross of Christ, mankind was divided into two groups: *Jews* and *Gentiles*. The Old and New Testaments both make very clear what caused this distinction: the everlasting covenants that God had made with Abraham, Isaac, and Jacob, and with their descendents through Moses. These covenants were *for Israel alone* and separated her from all other nations on the face of the earth (Lev. 20: 24-26), thereby making God's "chosen people" absolutely unique. [10] (emphasis mine)

Here Hunt recognizes the difference between Jews and gentiles "before the cross." Although he implies a change in that relationship after the cross, we still hear that God will have two peoples during both the Tribulation and the Millennium. In the Tribulation we hear of the saints. They say these are wedded to Christ while the saints of earth are suffering tribu-

lation. In the Millennium we hear that Israel will be
ruled by the Church. Another advocate of this kind of
future, when considering the Church's relationship to
Israel, argues:

> . . . I believe that the title **"the Israel of God"**
> refers to that believing remnant of ethnic Israel-
> ites who will be saved when the Messiah returns
> in His Second Advent. This agrees with Paul's
> most definitive teaching about the status of Israel
> in Romans chapters nine, ten, and eleven.[11]

But it becomes obvious that Lindsay is not completely sold on his argument. Listen as he continues:

> But just for the sake of argument, even if that
> passage did mean that the Church is the spiritual
> Israel of God in this age, it would in no way mean
> that ethnic Israel could not be restored to the
> national preeminence promised them in the
> unconditional covenants. [12]

My point is that not only is Israel to inherit the
promises, but the Church is joined to Israel in that
inheritance!

> I am the good shepherd; I know my own and my
> own know me, as the Father knows me and I
> know the Father; I lay down my life for the sheep.
> And I have other sheep [Gentiles], that are not of
> this fold [Israel]; I must bring them also, and they
> will heed my voice. So there will be one flock, and
> one shepherd. (Jn. 10: 14-16. Also see Deut. 29:
> 1-14)

This prophecy by our Messiah relates to His
coming to bring the New Covenant (Heb. 7:22; 8:13).
If this prophecy was to relate God's future plan for the
Jews and gentiles, and if it was fulfilled by Messiah
through the cross, as I believe and as Hunt implies,
then God, who devised this plan (unlike us, because

He changes not), had to begin with it and build upon it. The answer to the next question therefore is critical.

In the covenants, is there evidence that God intended to have one people integrated into the kingdom? I found that this was not an after-thought to God. In chapter 12 of Genesis, God made a promise to Abram, "I will make of you **a great nation**" (vs. 2). This statement is important for us to understand, for the land covenant which God later gave Abram in chapter 17 was different. Here He said that He would make of him "**a multitude of nations**"—not just one, as stated in chapter 12 where the promise was first given.

The reason for this difference is clear. For God, when He called Abram out of Ur of the Chaldees, had made a promise to make of him a great nation, which was **an eternal promise**, confirmed to Abraham in Genesis 17 and to us in Hebrews 11:8-16. Yet, God said that He would make up that **one eternal nation of promise** out of many nations from this present age. This was stated in the covenant itself, outlined in Genesis 17:1-8. In verse 4 we see the promise that Abram would be the father of a multitude of nations, but just how that one nation would relate was recorded in verse 8. The covenant or the promise that would someday be fulfilled in the new kingdom age would be to all of the descendants of Abraham, those who are the saved of the ages and who have populated the nations throughout this present age. Yet, in the end (in the kingdom age), these will be **one nation** made from the multitude of nations (vs. 8). There is no doubt that these nations will also include Israel.

> And I will give to your descendants after you, the land of your sojournings, all the land of Canaan, for an everlasting possession; and I will be their God.

And again in Micah we read:

> Therefore he shall give them up until the time
> when she who is in travail has brought forth; then
> the rest of his brethren shall return to the people
> of Israel. (Mic. 5:3)

It certainly appears from these promises that all of Abraham's descendents (heirs from every nation—not just the Jews) will some day take up residence in the promised land. If this is confirmed by the balance of Scripture, we then have an irrefutable truth. But is this not what Paul had said concerning us as gentile heirs of Abraham? Are we not now a part of the covenants ("no longer alienated"), and part of the commonwealth of Israel? (Eph. 2:12-13) Is this not why the writer of Hebrews (Heb. 8:10) and Paul's letters to the Romans (Rom. 4:13-17), confirm that even the New Covenant is with "the house of Israel"? And is this not also why Revelation makes the following statement?

> Worthy art thou to take the scroll and to open its
> seals, for thou wast slain and by thy blood didst
> ransom men for God from every tribe and tongue
> and people and nation, and hast made them a
> kingdom and priests to our God, and they shall
> reign on earth. (Rev. 5:9b.-10)

God's plan is for the one Church to be comprised of all saved Jews and gentiles. Any teaching which separates the Church from a future saved Israel is unscriptural, dividing the Church with a premature Rapture. The question, then, is: can we find scriptural confirmation showing why the Millennium must not be taken literally for this earth, and why the people of God must not be one during that period in the coming kingdom age (after the Church is complete). Although it is true that we find a separation of the Church and Israel taught dogmatically from the pulpits in our day, theologians recognize that there is no scriptural support, but only theory to back this.

The New Testament, because of the cross of Christ, makes believing gentiles and Jews equal heirs to the covenants as God's "chosen people." Therefore, unless we can find something in the New Testament to refute this in the Scriptures, then this union will not be reversed even in the kingdom. You are going to see that Scripture teaches mankind remains divided into two groups in the kingdom—the saved (those in Christ who are heirs to the covenants) and the unsaved (those outside of Christ and outside the covenant), but there is no division between the Church and Israel. The writer of Hebrews, when speaking of Christ's redemption, states, "For surely it is not with angels that he is concerned but with the descendents of Abraham" (Heb. 2:16).

I decided that if this premise is correct, then I had to question the current teaching of most dispensationalists on the Second Coming, because the teaching divides the people of the New Covenant. I felt that I had to dig into the Scriptures, which are said to teach a rapture prior to the end of the Tribulation. This search led to answers for many of the questions which had arisen while sitting under various dispensationalist teachers. These issues have been resolved in my own mind. You will need to be the judge of what is presented here. Does the thinking which follows present a literal interpretation of Scripture and remain true to the people of the covenants? Does it answer from Scripture our questions, rather than create questions that seemingly have no answer? Does the Scripture actually teach a separation of the Church and Israel during the Great Tribulation?

TWO

*WHAT IS TAUGHT—
HOW ARE WE
TO TEST IT?*

In this book you'll find many references to the Jehovah's Witnesses, which will be used as an example of "how not to". I will do this not because they are your greatest enemy, but because what they have done with Scripture many of our fundamentalist and evangelical leaders have also unknowingly done in our day. No, not intentionally—but, they have done it nonetheless. Let me give you just a flavor of what I have found being taught in recent days. As I was teaching a class on this subject, there were those who were questioning clear statements of Scripture based upon teachings contained in a book by Grant Jeffrey. Within its pages, Jeffrey writes concerning Matthew 24 (the passage spoken to earlier), saying:

> One of the classic mistakes in interpretation is to take this conversation between Christ and His Jewish disciples concerning the Messianic Kingdom and read back into it the reality of the Christian Church . . .[1]

In this section of his book, Jeffrey places a great deal of distinction on the disciples as Jews versus their being a part of the Church. All of this might sound reasonable, as I'm sure it must have to some of my students, but consider the following: at the upper room during the last week of Christ's earthly ministry (just after the Mount Olivet discourse spoken of above by Jeffrey), the Lord made the following statement to His Jewish disciples: "... Where I am going you cannot come. A new commandment I give to you, love one another; even as I have loved you, that you also love one another. By this all men will know that you are my disciples, if you have love for one another." Now, immediately after this we read that Peter asked the Lord a question: "Lord, where are you going?" and Jesus answered, "... I go to prepare a place for you. And when I go and prepare a place for you, I will come again and will take you to myself, that where I am, you may be also." Jesus went on to tell His **Jewish disciples** that they know the way to where He would be going. "Jesus said [to them], 'I am the way, and the truth, and the life; no one comes to the Father, but by me.'"

You might be asking what this has to do with Jeffrey's reasoning. Consider: if Matthew 24 is only for the Jewish nation because the Lord Jesus spoke it to His **Jewish disciples**, then what Jesus said to His Jewish disciples in John 13 and 14 must also be meant only for the nation Israel. Thus, we could conclude that Jesus is only coming back to rapture the nation Israel. I would merely ask that you consider all of the facts before making up your mind. I'm going to present the scriptural facts as best I can in the pages to follow.

Lest you think that I'm too negative concerning my brother, let me just say that Jeffrey has uncovered many interesting points concerning the timing surrounding end-time prophecies. These I will certainly consider in my own future study about just when the Great Tribulation could possibly occur. I certainly

hope that Jeffrey will do the same with the material
that you are about to read. We all have to remember
that no one of us is perfect, and I hope that we are all
looking for the truth!

As you'll discover, I found that Scripture does
not clearly teach as truth the doctrine of a rapture
seven years prior to Christ's coming to earth. Yet, the
adherents to this doctrinal position would have us
believe otherwise. Most of the evangelical and fundamentalist branches of the Church today see the Second Coming of the Lord being in two separate stages.
They say that the Church will be gone when the
Tribulation begins, and in fact this will be a direct
cause of the turmoil that leads to the "Great Tribulation." This secret disappearance, it's taught, will cause
confusion on earth due to the void left by the disappearance of millions of Christians.

Dave Hunt, who agrees with Jeffrey on the timing
of the Rapture, says when speaking of these same
verses in Matthew 24:

> This scripture is commonly presented as abso-
> lute proof for a post-tribulation rapture. That
> would be the case, however, only if it refers to
> Christ's coming to take the church to heaven. On
> the other hand, if it is describing Christ's second
> coming to rescue Israel, which indeed it is, then
> this Scripture is not teaching a post-tribulation
> rapture at all.[2]

Dave Hunt also applies these verses to Israel. He
says that Israel will not be raptured. Rather, her saints
will be resurrected to possess the Promised Land. He
says that it is the Church only who is promised the
Rapture, yet this passage is speaking of the Rapture:
"For as the lightning comes from the east and shines
as far as the west, so will be the coming of the Son of
Man. Wherever the body is, there the eagles will be
gathered together." This must speak of the Rapture,

for where "the body [Christ's body] is there [in the air]
the eagles will be." Why else would the Lord say this?
He's warning about false christs, and about the loca-
tion of those false christs. Yet the true Christ will call
us to Himself in the air. He is saying if you understand
this, you'll not be deceived!

Hunt further states:

> While entire books have been written against
> the pre-trib rapture, no argument can nullify
> the major reasons we have given for its neces-
> sity: 1) The *pre-tribulation rapture* is the *only*
> event that could conceivably cause the world
> to unite under and to worship the Antichrist
> . . . 2) the *pre-trib rapture* is essential to remove
> the restraining influence of the Holy Spirit
> operating in Christians and thereby give the
> Antichrist the free hand he must have: and 3)
> the *pre-trib rapture* is *necessary* because . . . only
> by removal of the church can two prophecies
> both be fulfilled that would otherwise be in
> hopeless conflict: a) that the Antichrist will
> have complete power over all of earth's inhab-
> itants, including "saints," and will kill all who
> refuse to worship him, and b) that the gates of
> hell will not prevail against the church.[3]

Although points one and two will be dealt with
elsewhere in this book, I would like to look for a
moment at the third of Hunt's arguments. In Revelation 13, the beast from the sea is given power to
conquer and to kill those who do not receive the mark
of the beast. Hunt indicates that this would constitute
the gates of hell prevailing over the Church, were the
Church to still be here. Did the Lord really mean this
as Hunt concludes? God never promised that we
would conquer death in this mortal flesh, but that it

would be conquered for us as He gives us immortality. Satan has won many battles, but to win a battle is not to prevail!

Also to conclude that all saints will be killed during the tribulation is a misconception. There is no definite proof in the Revelation that all saints will suffer death. Israel, who will be saved at the end of the tribulation, as an example, will not suffer death before the Lord returns. The 144,000 sealed of Israel are included with the saints by even the pre-tribulationists. Hunt's arguments hold no water—there is no hopeless conflict within these two statements as they are seen by those who believe that we might be here.

I will make you one promise. We will not make statements criticizing others' beliefs without digging into the issues at hand. We will be looking at the Scriptures line upon line. There are various teachings undergirding the view of a rapture prior to tribulation. These teachings, in order to be true, must be firmly supported by Scripture. In order to understand what Scripture teaches on this subject, we'll examine the makeup of each of the more popular teachings in light of scripture. You're probably familiar with each of them, but it would be good to review them here:

FIRST. The Bible teaches a catching away of believers who are alive and remain when Christ comes, following the first resurrection. This teaching is solid, but when will it occur? It's taught that this is to occur in conjunction with the time established in Revelation 4:1, with the sounding of the trumpet recorded there. This trumpet is said to be the last trumpet to sound for the Church. If this is correct, the Church and Israel will be two peoples at least throughout the Millennium, and the facts of our premise will be confused.

SECOND. God has not appointed the Church to WRATH (again a solid scriptural teaching)! But is the Great Tribulation the wrath that God has promised to keep us from? This is the current teaching.

THIRD. Most theologians say that Paul teaches in (2 Thess. 2) that the Church must be out of the way before the Antichrist can appear. This reasoning ties the Holy Spirit and the Church together as a restraining force holding back his appearing. Is this correct?

FOURTH. Under the two-part coming theory, He would come once as a thief, and once in the clouds—once *for* His saints (called the Rapture of the Church), and once *with* His saints (returning to the earth in what is known as the "revelation of Christ"). But the question is: are these distinctions in terms recorded within the pages of Scripture meant to teach two stages of the Second Coming?

FIFTH. Many who hold this theory see the promise to the church of Philadelphia as a promise to the entire Church, to keep it from the hour of trial or testing; as being a promise to rapture the Church prior to the Great Tribulation. But, will this promise be fulfilled by means of the rapture?

SIXTH. Since the word "church" does not appear after chapter 3 of Revelation, it's taught that this is evidence that the Church is no longer present on earth during the Great Tribulation. Is this a proper conclusion, in light of the fact that the saints are yet present in and during the Tribulation period?

SEVENTH. The Church is to expect the imminent return of Christ. This teaching states that Christ could have returned at any moment in history. Is this true according to Scripture?

EIGHTH. Many see dispensations or time periods in which God deals differently with man. It is said that the Tribulation is one such dispensation, and that it's related to Daniel's seventieth week, a time of dealing with a special people (Israel). The times of the gentiles must then be complete and therefore the Church is gone. It's during this time that the marriage supper of the Lamb is said to occur, which creates further justification for a rapture prior to the Tribulation. It's also at this time that the judgement of the raptured Church is said to occur. Is this teaching supported by Scripture? When does the Scripture teach that the Church will be judged?

All of this teaching taken together makes a believable argument on the surface. It also left for me many unanswered questions when compared with the actual Scriptures which supposedly teach these things! Here in the pages that follow, we will look at each of these teachings separately. We'll dig deep and we'll find that there are problems with each of these areas when we attempt to compare them with Scripture in order to prove the Rapture prior to the end of the Tribulation.

Perhaps you're asking what some of the problems are in our current popular teachings? If you'll allow me, I'll list just a few of them for you:

1. If the Church is a separate dispensation and the Church apart from Israel is the Bride of Christ, then why do we see Israel, the Church, and the saved of Revelation all spoken of as the saints within Scripture?

2. Why do we not have a good explanation for sacrifice during the Millennium?

3. What is God's eternal plan for Israel? In other words, how can God have two separate peoples? Are they separate, and if so what's the basis for their separation? Is it the covenants; and if so, how do the covenants explain this separation?

4. Is Old Testament Israel represented by those men and women of faith a part of the Bride or a part of the nation Israel, if these two are separate? If we are the children of faith under Abraham, just where do they fit?

5. Why do the parables teach a gathering of both

the evil and the good at the same time if the Rapture is to occur seven, or even three-and-one-half years, prior to the battle of Armageddon?

6. Why do born-again Christians view the Second Coming differently, with some seeing Tribulation with no Millennium, and others seeing a Millennium with no Tribulation?

7. Is this confusion of the Lord or of Satan?

These aren't all of the questions.

THREE

WHEN DOES THE LAST TRUMPET SOUND?

In search of the last trumpet!

A search for the trumpet that is to catch us away would be a proper place to begin our search for scriptural truths. First, is there scriptural evidence to support the popular teaching that the Rapture occurs in Revelation 4:1? Second, is the trumpet that is said to sound in this passage the trumpet that will call us home?

The scriptural support for the Rapture's occurrence is based on Paul's teaching on the resurrection of the dead. For Paul the apostle spoke of the mystery of this moment (the moment when the Rapture is actually to occur) in 1 Cor. 15:51-54, with excitement:

> Lo! I tell you a mystery. We shall not all sleep, but we shall all be changed, in a moment, in the twinkling of an eye, at the last trumpet. For the trumpet will sound, and the dead will be raised imperishable, and we shall be changed. For the perishable nature must put on imperishable, and the mortal nature must put on immortality, . . . then shall come to pass the saying that is written: "Death is swallowed up in victory."

41

In this passage, Paul describes in explicit detail these events, and it becomes obvious that this mystery is the Rapture of the Church. He also spoke of it again in 1 Thessalonians 4:13-18.

> But we would not have you ignorant, brethren, concerning those who are asleep, that you may not grieve as others do who have no hope. For since we believe that Jesus died and rose again, even so, through Jesus, God will bring with him those who have fallen asleep. For this we declare to you by the word of the Lord, that we who are alive who are left until the coming of the Lord shall not precede those who have fallen asleep. For the Lord himself will descend from heaven with a cry of command, with the archangel's call, and with the sound of the trumpet of God. And the dead in Christ will rise first; then we who are alive, who are left, shall be caught up together with them in the CLOUDS to meet the Lord in the air; and so we shall always be with the Lord. Therefore comfort one another with these words.

Now, in both passages Paul mentions the sound of the trumpet that will call us home. If we look to Rev. 4:1 to the place in Scripture where this event is said to occur (placing it before the Tribulation), then we'll see that John said he heard a voice "speaking to me like a trumpet" which said "Come up hither." It's easy to conclude from the context that this voice was speaking to John and inviting him into the heavenlies. However, this trumpet heard by John is not a trumpet at all, but merely an angel speaking "like a trumpet." Scripture shows that there is an actual trumpet sounded in both passages where Paul describes this event, BUT NO ACTUAL TRUMPET in Revelation 4:1.

If we're to give Revelation 4:1 any place in this event, we would have to consider that there must be a hidden interpretation of this Scripture that takes special revelation and understanding. What we see here in Revelation 4:1 has a different emphasis altogether from what Paul had described surrounding the Rapture.

But there's additional evidence which caused me to conclude that this could be erroneous interpretation. Let's return to 1 Cor. 15:51-54. Here Paul says that the catching away will occur at a particular time (the last trumpet). Now what does that mean? In Revelation we see listed seven trumpets to be sounded after this event listed in chapter 4, verse 1. We should ask ourselves what makes this event qualify as the last trumpet when there is an actual last trumpet recorded in chapters 10 and 11?

Now, you need to understand that many dispensationalists deny that the seven trumpets of Revelation chapters 8-11 have anything to do with the Rapture. This is interesting, since these same teachers identify the Feast of Trumpets, and even the trumpets which were blown in the wilderness, with the Rapture. Hal Lindsay speaks of the seven trumpets of the Old Testament, and yet in the end ignored the seven trumpets of Revelation. In speaking about the timing of the Rapture, Lindsay states:

> This will take place "at the last trumpet," which refers to something which was the practice of God in the Old Testament. When the Israelites were on their march from Egypt over to the land of Palestine, every morning before they started on their journey, they would have seven trumpets blow—to prepare to brake camp, fold up their tents, etc. When the seventh trumpet, *which was the last trumpet*, sounded, this meant—move out! The idea in this passage is that when God has the last trumpet blow it means He will move out all the Christians—and at that point we shall be changed.[1] (emphasis mine)

Lindsay recognizes the trumpets, and then records a question which immediately follows the above statement. In it he asks: "What's in a word?"[2] We of course could ask the same question. Just exactly what's in the word "seventh" as it relates to the last trumpet? If the last trumpet blast is the time of the catching away of the church as Paul literally states, then just when does this last trumpet take place?

In order to arrive at the answer we're going to look to Revelation 11: 15-19:

> Then the seventh angel blew his trumpet, and there were loud voices in heaven saying, "The kingdom of the world has become the kingdom of our Lord and of his Christ, and he shall reign for ever and ever." And the twenty-four elders who sit on their thrones before God fell on their faces and worshiped God, saying, "We give thanks to thee, Lord God Almighty, who art and who wast, that thou hast taken thy great power and begun to reign. The nations raged, but thy wrath came, and the time for the dead to be judged, for rewarding thy servants, the prophets and saints, and those who fear thy name, both small and great, and for destroying the destroyers of the earth." Then God's temple in heaven was opened, and the ark of his covenant was seen within his temple; and there were flashes of lightning, voices, peals of thunder, an earthquake, and heavy hail.

It becomes apparent from these verses that what is depicted here is a climax to the events of history as we know it. The announcement sure sounds much more like Paul's description of the Rapture. The event is announced with loud voices. We see that Christ has begun to reign. We also see that its the time for the dead to be judged, and the servants of God to be rewarded. "The kingdom of this world has become the

kingdom of the Lord and of his Christ and he shall
reign forever." It should be recognized here that there
are those who see this as being the middle of the seven-
year tribulation. The reason for this comes as a result
of the positioning of this event directly in the middle
of Revelation.

There are a few important things that we need to
understand from this prophecy. One of the major
events described here in connection with the Lord's
coming is the judgment of the dead, and in order for
the dead to be judged, there must be a resurrection
accompanying it.

There is more that we need to understand surrounding this event. We need, also, to consider the
mystery connected to the Rapture. The seventh trumpet or last trumpet to be sounded in Revelation is
introduced in Rev. 10: 7 with these words: "but that in
the last days of the trumpet call to be sounded by the
seventh angel, the mystery of God as he announced it
to his servants the prophets should be fulfilled."

The question which immediately became apparent in my mind when reading this passage was this: is
the mystery recorded here in Revelation 10 the same
mystery that Paul spoke of in 1 Cor. 15:51? Certainly
Revelation 10 is speaking of something being revealed
that would remain a mystery up until the sounding of
the seventh trumpet. Paul's mystery was the resurrection itself. The point here is that a resurrection occurs
with the sounding of the seventh trumpet.

It certainly appeared that this mystery and the
one recorded in Revelation could be one and the same
mystery. One thing is sure—there will be no more
delay. The mystery of Revelation was about to be
revealed at the sounding of this last trumpet recorded
in Revelation 10:6. And we certainly know, because
the Lord will begin to reign after its sounding, that the
resurrection by this time will have occurred. We also

know that there was no mention of a mystery being revealed nor of a resurrection having occurred in Rev. 4:1. But it's the other scriptural proof that I later discovered which reveals that this was the actual time of the resurrection and rapture.

There is one other important area to consider, the Feast of Trumpets mentioned in Leviticus 23: 23-25. Trumpets were blown to mark the end of whatever was occurring in Israel at the time, and the beginning of a day of rest. We consider the Millennium as the day of rest. Bible scholars see the many major events involving God's prophetic plan as being revealed in the feasts of the Old Testament. Many of these same scholars say that there's no actual Old Testament feast to identify with a pre-tribulational rapture. They don't see the Rapture identified within the feasts as a separate event, even though they consider it to be a separate event. They instead tie the Rapture and Second Coming into one feast, the Feast of Trumpets.

It is my belief that these trumpets represent the seven trumpets of Revelation. But there is even further proof in the feasts for a rapture following the Tribulation. We do have a separate identifier within the prophetic feasts of the Old Testament for the Rapture. It could be argued that the Feast of Harvest would identify with the Rapture. It certainly seems clear that harvest goes along with the purpose of the Rapture, for then all of the fruit of the gospel will be gathered. The actual feast which represents this portion of the harvest at the end of the age is called the Feast of Ingathering. Exodus records what the Lord had commanded Israel regarding these feasts associated with harvest. "You shall keep the feast of harvest, of the first fruits of your labor, of what you sow in the field. You shall keep the feast of ingathering at the end of the year, when you gather in from the field the fruit of your labor" (Exod.23:16). The first feast of harvest

(First Fruits) was fulfilled by the Lord at His resurrection, according to Dr. Willmington of Liberty University.[3] Yet, he makes no mention of the significance of the Feast of Ingathering. It would certainly seem that if the Feast of First Fruits refers to Christ's resurrection (1 Cor. 15:20-23), then the last feast (ingathering) will be fulfilled at the time of the Rapture or resurrection of the saints.

The actual meaning for ingathering is ignored by most who have written on this feast. Ingathering was celebrated by Israel at the time of the seven-day celebration of the Feast of Booths. Its significance to the dispensational theologian is that it points to the Millennium. And indeed it does, but the very thing necessary to bring in the Millennium is the ingathering (the Rapture). There are two other important points concerning this feast. It is to be celebrated for one week. And since the Lord says that it is a celebration of ingathering of harvest, which is to occur at the end of the year, there is then no one day that can be pointed to for the harvest or Rapture to occur. "No man knoweth the day or the hour" of our Lord's coming!

Also based on the Lord's command (to celebrate the harvest at the end of the year after it is complete), if the Rapture had already occurred, our celebration would need to begin in heaven with the wedding feast at the end of the year of the Rapture. And since this would leave Tribulation saints who will be resurrected later completely out of the harvest, this would create a conflict with the Lord's command to celebrate after the harvest or ingathering.

FOUR

WHAT IS THE WRATH OF GOD?

> Behold, the storm of the Lord! Wrath has gone forth, a whirling tempest; it will burst upon the head of the wicked. The anger of the Lord will not turn back until he has executed and accomplished the intents of his mind. In the latter days you will understand it clearly. (Jer. 23:19-20)

The Bible speaks of a day which is coming when God will punish all ungodly men. This day is known as the day of wrath. There has been an argument presented to the Church in our day in support of the Rapture happening prior to the Tribulation. The argument is that God has not appointed the Church to wrath, and the Tribulation is the time of God's wrath! This argument seeks its support from Paul's teaching in 1 Thess. 5:9, "For God has not destined us for wrath, but to obtain salvation through our Lord Jesus Christ." The wrath that he speaks of here is identified by some popular teachers of our day with the Great Tribulation. Is it?

When God's wrath occurs in Scripture, it is a matter of urgency that men act or be destroyed. Moses knew that there was urgency here, for the wrath of God had gone forth.[1]

Nahum gave a description of God's wrath. "The Lord takes vengeance on his adversaries and keeps wrath for his enemies" (Nah. 1:2). Listen again to what Nahum says concerning man's ability to sustain God's wrath. "Who can stand before his indignation? Who can endure the heat of his anger? His wrath is poured out like fire, and the rocks are broken asunder by him" (Nah. 1:6).

The problem is, though, that evil men still remain on this earth after the Tribulation period is concluded. Does this mean that during the Tribulation God's wrath missed its target? Apparently those who believe that God must rapture the Church before the Tribulation must also believe that God's wrath can go astray and inflict injury indiscriminately. The Rapture is not necessary for God to protect His Church.

So, if the Church must be raptured to avoid God's wrath, what will happen to the saved of the Tribulation? Apparently, persons saved during the Tribulation would suffer God's wrath simply because they are present during this time. We have here a real dilemma. It could possibly be argued that if God's purpose is to save the Church from wrath by means of the Rapture, then the effect will be to punish the saved of the Tribulation because they missed the Rapture. After the Rapture it would appear that all men will pay for their sin, having rejected Christ.

There were several other reasons why I had serious questions in my mind. If the Tribulation is the day of God's wrath, then the two witnesses of Revelation, who we are taught (by many) will be Elijah and Moses, are out of place in God's plan, and therefore a contradiction exists. We see these witnesses in Revelation occupying the last three-and-one-half years of the Tribulation period (Rev. 11:1-3). This obviously is the Tribulation, for it fits the events and extends for the same duration of time as the Tribulation. Yet, when we

look into Scripture to see when Elijah is supposed to
come as described in Malachi 4:5, we find that he can't
possibly be here at this time. "Behold, I will send you
Elijah the prophet before the great and terrible day of
the LORD comes." If Elijah is to come before the Day
of the Lord, then the Tribulation can't be the day of
wrath. The Day of the Lord is spoken of many places
as a terrible day—a day of darkness, a day of wrath. I
believe that Elijah is in fact one of the two witnesses.
Even pre-tribulational theology gives good scriptural
argument for this fact. Elijah had never seen death,
since he was caught up in a chariot of fire. Because it
is appointed unto man once to die, and since the two
witnesses will see death, it would seem that Elijah is a
logical candidate to be one of these two witnesses. If
these dispensationalists are right on the identity of
Elijah, then they are wrong on the timing of the day of
wrath. In other words, if this is the Tribulation, they
have Elijah present during the Tribulation, which
Malachi 4:5 indicates is not the case.

You might be thinking, just what's the purpose of
Paul's statement concerning wrath in I Thess. 5:9 if
these things are true? It is obvious that the wrath of
God recorded in the Bible is aimed at the judgment of
the wicked, and it often occurs when godly people are
present. This judgment is never aimed at the people of
God unless they deliberately disobey. The New Testament description is no different than the Old in this
regard. All passages in Scripture speak of God's wrath
in the same way—all identify it with the judgment of the
wicked. One possible fly in the ointment is Romans
2:8-9, which seems to link wrath and tribulation, but its
point is not the Tribulation; it instead is demonstrat-
ing the universal consequences of rebellion against
God.

The Holy Spirit has not left us without explanation of wrath, one which is helpful in our own under-

standing of just what Paul is saying in 1 Thess. 5:9.
First, consider where Paul speaks of our life apart from
Christ, ". . .we were by nature children of wrath, like
the rest of mankind."[2] This Scripture certainly makes
a definite statement concerning the objects of wrath.
Second, in Eph. 5:5-6, we see the following: "Be sure
of this, that no fornicator or impure man, or one who
is covetous (that is, an idolater), has an inheritance in
the kingdom of Christ and of God. Let no one deceive
you with empty words, for it is because of these things
that the wrath of God comes upon the sons of disobe-
dience." This verse again makes another plain statement of the meaning that Paul had in mind when he
wrote concerning God's wrath. It implies judgment,
and again we have seen just who it would be who would
receive it. We also see how Paul describes to the
Thessalonians the wrath of God. Here he doesn't use
the actual word "wrath," but his meaning is clear, as he
says: ". . . when the Lord Jesus is revealed from heaven
with his mighty angels in flaming fire, inflicting vengeance upon those who do not know God and upon
those who do not obey the gospel of our Lord Jesus.
They shall suffer the punishment of eternal destruction and exclusion from the presence of the Lord and
from the glory of his might . . ."[3] Here Paul even tells
us when this wrath will occur, and he tells us that it is
an eternal punishment.

At the final judgement of man mentioned in Rev.
20:7-17, we see God's wrath in action. Yet in the earlier
Scriptures recorded here, it became clear that there is
a wrath to be poured out on the earth immediately
after the Lord returns, and this wrath will not await
final judgment: "Then the kings of the earth and the
great men and the generals and the rich and the
strong, and every one, slave and free, hid in the caves
and among the rocks . . . and cried 'Fall on us and hide
us from the face of Him who is seated on the throne,

and from the wrath of the Lamb; for the great day of their wrath has come, and who can stand before it?" (Rev. 6:15-17).

"And another angel, a third, followed them, saying with a loud voice, 'If any one worships the beast and its image, and receives a mark on his forehead or on his hand, he also shall drink the wine of God's wrath, poured unmixed into the cup of his anger, . . . in the presence of the Lamb" (Rev. 14:9-10).

These Scriptures not only reveal the truth concerning whom against God's wrath will be poured out, but they also reveal another most interesting point—the Lamb will be present at this outpouring of God's wrath. Listen as Zechariah describes this day: "Then the Lord will go forth and fight against those nations as when He fights on the day of battle. On that day His feet shall stand on the Mount of Olives which lies before Jerusalem on the east" (Zech. 14:3-4a.). It is clear that this wrath is after the Tribulation when the Lord is present on this earth, and not during it, as we are taught by any two-part-coming theory. It's true that Tribulation saints will suffer persecution, but this obviously comes from Satan, not from God.[4] In other words, not God's wrath that is bringing torment and even death into these lives. God, in fact, commends the saints for their suffering and offers them a special place in the coming kingdom.

What happens to the Church during the Tribulation?

As we've seen previously, the Tribulation period involves but is not equivalent to God's wrath; therefore the purpose for wrath must be different than the purpose for the Tribulation. We might then ask, "just what is the purpose for the Tribulation?" The Lord calls it "the hour of trial . . . to try those who dwell upon the earth" (Rev. 3:10).

God's judgment will begin to be poured out

upon the wicked of the world at this time, but the purpose is not total destruction of the world. We see the sealing of the saints in Rev. 7:3. We see the multitude of those who have come out of the Great Tribulation, those who have washed their robes and made them white in the blood of the Lamb (Rev. 7:14). There are those even in the midst of destruction who will give glory to the God of heaven (Rev. 11: 13). The hour of testing is to test the saints, as well as the world and the enemies of the Church (Rev. 12:17; 13:10; 14:12). It is important not to overlook the fact that in the midst of all of the upheaval, the gospel is also being sent out to the entire earth (Rev. 14:6-7).

In this age, judgment is always intended to turn people back to God. Unity will be brought about during the Great Tribulation. Tribulation from without has always been a unifying force for the Church, and judgment, we are told, begins with the household of God. Unfortunate though this may seem, it is God's Word. The Great Tribulation will bring this force to bear on the entire Church for the first time since its early persecution by Rome.

The fact that judgment begins with the Church could mean that the Church needs to be purged. There is coming a time of purging and testing within the Church, for the holy people of God will see the Great Tribulation.[5] The Lord will use Satan and his wrath to separate the wheat from the chaff during this time of testing. No man or woman living at that time will escape the effects of the Great Tribulation. God's saints, those who endure to the end either through death or through God's protection, will escape His wrath, but not His judgment! If tribulation involves only wrath, then none would be saved. Yet we know that the Lord will shorten the days so that the faithful will be saved and the Church completed. The final completion of the Church will be accomplished when

Israel repents, accepting her Messiah. Thus the people of the New Covenant will be complete.

In Romans we find that Paul confirms this truth. He mentions in 11:15 "life from the dead" when speaking of the coming salvation of the nation Israel. This is talking about the resurrection, which is associated with Israel's day of salvation, which will occur in the midst of wrath. John Walvoord has this to say about this passage.

> Because Paul was convinced that Israel's stumbling is temporary, he asked, **What will their acceptance be but life from the dead** (lit., "out from dead ones")? This question explains the clause, "How much greater riches will their fullness bring" (v. 12). Israel's "acceptance" of Christ is related to "the first resurrection." (Rev. 20:4-6)[6]

Some dispensationalists attempt to create several resurrections all as part of the first resurrection of the just. However, Paul in 1 Corinthians 15 spoke of only one. But, because some see more than one, we still must ask, "Who this resurrection is to include?" We learn from this passage that Israel had been cut off so that you and I could be blessed. Our blessing comes from our inclusion in the New Covenant. Paul was teaching that resurrection (life from the dead) will come to all of us who have received the blessing of the New Covenant, when Israel accepts this same covenant for herself. She will at that time accept what she had originally rejected as a nation, and her acceptance will bring about the resurrection for all saints. "Lo! I tell you a mystery. We shall not all sleep, but we shall all be changed, in a moment, in the twinkling of an eye, at the last trumpet."[7] There is only one future resurrection recorded in Scripture for the saints! And that resurrection will come before the outpouring of wrath known as the day of wrath, which is also known as the Day of the Lord (Zeph. 1:14-15).

When considering wrath, we must realize that there have always been occasions of God's wrath poured out on evil men. The fact that wrath is present during the Tribulation does not make the Tribulation period equal the Day of the Lord. Let's summarize what we see concerning the Day of the Lord (the day of wrath) from God's eyes:

—First, from Zechariah 14 we see that "the Day of the Lord" has the Lord going forth to fight against the nations surrounding Jerusalem. And "on that day his feet shall stand on the Mount of Olives."

—Second, in Revelation 16:12–16, "the great day of God the Almighty" sees the whole world assembled for battle, and the Lord announcing, "Lo, I am coming like a thief! Blessed is he who is awake."

—Third, 1 Thessalonians 5:2–4 says, "The Day of the Lord will come like a thief in the night. When people say, 'peace and security,' then sudden destruction will come upon them as travail comes upon a woman with child, and there will be no escape. But you are not in darkness, brethren, for that day to surprise you like a thief." Peace and security is the cry of the age, and many believe that it will come about through the annihilation of Christians and Jews. Men will see the battle of Armageddon as the final step toward peace and security. Russell Chandler in his book states that "according to . . .UFO logists . . . cosmic intelligences have come . . . to guide us into the New Age, . . . this will cause birth pangs, but once reached, this higher state will only be the beginning of a golden age of peace and prosperity." [8]

—Fourth, in 2 Thessalonians 2:1-4 Paul says, "Don't be shaken" or "excited . . . to the effect that the day of the Lord has come." He further warns that we are not to let men deceive us, for that Day will not come unless rebellion comes, and Antichrist proclaims himself to be God.

—Fifth, Satan will be punished on that day, and the dragon that is in the sea will be slain (Isa. 27:1). "And then that lawless one . . . the Lord will slay . . . by his appearing and his coming" (2 Thess. 2:8).

—Sixth, The Lord alone will be exalted in that Day (Isa. 2:11). The Tribulation will exalt the Antichrist, not the Lord.

—Seventh, He is coming to be glorified in His saints on that day (2 Thess. 1:10). If any man can read these verses and proclaim that the Day of the Lord is the Tribulation—he is confused!! Knowing all of this, can we adopt a position that the Church must be removed during a time when the Holy Spirit intends to do His final work within the Church, just because we are not destined for God's wrath? I have to conclude that the answer from Scripture also is NO, for God's wrath does not render the Tribulation useless to God.

FIVE

IS THE CHURCH INSTRUMENTAL IN RESTRAINING THE EVIL ONE?

"The Church is an instrument used by the Spirit in restraining of evil. With the rapture, not a single believer will be left, and the Spirit's ministry of restraining will cease." [1]

The above statement spoken by Thiessen derives its support from 2 Thessalonians 2. Walvoord and Zuck, when writing on this passage, state that the Holy Spirit working through the Church makes up a force which holds back the Antichrist. They ask: "How does He [the Holy Spirit] do it? Through Christians, whom He indwells. . . ." (They continue): "How will He be **taken out of the way**? When the Church leaves the earth in the Rapture . . ." [2]

The apostle Paul states in this chapter (2 Thess. 2), in very plain language, the fact that the Second Coming will not occur until certain things are accomplished. His purpose for writing this passage is to keep the reader from becoming confused.

2 Thessalonians chapter 2 does not support a rapture of the Church prior to the Tribulation. Almost

everyone is agreed that Paul is speaking here of our Lord's coming to set up his kingdom. But those who believe in a rapture prior to the Tribulation say that this passage is not just referring to the Rapture. They say that verses 1–4 instead refer to the second stage of the Lord's coming (the "revelation" stage). It isn't until we come to the section concerning the removal of the restrainer that (they say) we will begin to deal with the Rapture. In other words, even though Paul's purpose was to eliminate confusion, unless we understand that the Second Coming occurs in two parts, we can't understand this passage. Nowhere in Paul's writings, or in any other Scripture for that matter, is there a single passage to inform us of these two parts. We who don't see this as two events are considered unlearned in Scripture. Perhaps we should be seen as unlearned so that we can clear up the confusion. Within this passage, Paul states concerning this son of perdition, that "he who now restrains it will do so until he is out of the way." The passage makes no mention of who the restrainer is, but verse 6 says "And you know what is restraining him." The Scripture is almost saying that it should be obvious to us what it is that is actually restraining the Antichrist. Is it the Church, as we're told?

Does past history show that God has used the Church in this capacity over the course of history? Where the Church has been present in power, evil in reaction has also reared its ugly head in persecution. The first century Church was thus far the most powerful in history, yet this was also the period of greatest persecution throughout all of church history. If anything, Satan rose up against the Church as a *response to* it, trying to restrain it. God is the Prime Mover and First Cause in history; Satan reacts.

Even beyond this, we can clearly see that the Church itself is powerless without the Holy Spirit.

There is no question that this power, if used by the Church, can be an effective force against evil. However, we're told that the world would wax worse and worse. Its effects will even be felt within the Church itself until there will be a concern for even the very elect of God. The Lord put it this way, "when the Son of Man comes will he find faith on earth?" (Luke 18:8). Obviously, as we read Revelation, we see that there is faith (great faith), but certainly the Lord's concern also shows us the seriousness of the world's impact on all men. Today there is evidence everywhere that this also should be the concern of the Church. Can a Church that has become more powerless than powerful be credited with restraining the evil one? I think not!

As I stated before, the restrainer is to be obvious to those of us in the faith. The only force that is obviously more powerful in our world than the evil one is the One in whom we put our trust every day. The Lord Jesus was at the beginning with God the Father and is credited in Scripture with the creation of all things. Yet, even Jesus himself said that He was not privileged to know the day or the hour of His coming. That places God the Father in complete control of future events. One day the Father will direct the Holy Spirit to remove restraint from the evil one, and the Antichrist will be revealed. However, Scripture does not show that the Church is raptured before the Antichrist is loosed to accomplish what he intends to do. "For the time is coming when people will not endure sound teaching, but having itching ears they will accumulate for themselves teachers to suit their own likings" (2 Tim. 4:3).

A second theory concerning the restrainer is that he is the Holy Spirit himself. Since the Holy Spirit is removed from the scene to allow Satan to work, this means that the Church must also be removed, because

the Holy Spirit indwells every believer. Let's consider
this theory: what would happen if the Holy Spirit were
removed from the earth? Certainly, the Antichrist
would have freedom to do anything he desired. But
without the Holy Spirit, no flesh can be saved. It
becomes apparent from Revelation 4-19 that there are
many saved during the Tribulation. Theology which
calls for a rapture prior to the Tribulation has to have
an answer for this.

One explanation is that during the Tribulation
we'll revert back to the law, and men will be saved by
what God will do therefore in the future for them. The
work of the Holy Spirit, they say, becomes like that of
his Old Testament workings.

The removal goes against the very character and
nature of God. God is omnipresent; He is present
everywhere and at all times. This presence is accomplished by His Spirit. Additionally, the Holy Spirit
must perform other work during the Tribulation
which only He can perform. Witnesses will be empow-
ered, miracles will take place, saints will be ministered
to. In thinking about this further, this teaching completely voids the work of Christ in salvation, and
reverts backward to the law. This almost seems blas-
phemous in light of the entire message of the gospel.

David Lurie, when writing on the 70th week of
Daniel, outlined the thinking of the dispensationalist
which makes this interpretation necessary in their
mind. He writes:

> According to this view, the seventieth week will
> be the water shed between two successive dispen-
> sations, the Church Age and the Millennial King-
> dom, and it will begin after the removal of the
> church . . . in the "pretribulational rapture." The
> removal of the church is necessary,
> dispensationalists believe, in order to allow
> Israel's restoration to proceed. Because the Cross

has broken down the "middle wall of partition" between Jew and Gentile (Eph. 2:14) there can be no distinction between Jew and Gentile in God's redemptive plan as long as the Church Age lasts. And because dispensationalists believe that Israel's restoration *would* create such a distinction, Israel can therefore not be restored until after the Church Age is brought to an end.[3]

If we accept this muddled thinking, we're in fact saying that Israel can be saved apart from Christ's redemptive work. Most pastors would not support this as being correct, yet they support the doctrine that requires this to be so. We know that Israel can't be saved apart from Christ's redemptive work, which requires the presence and working of the Holy Spirit. Remember the promise of the New Covenant was to Israel. Her salvation as a nation will not occur apart from this covenant, and Christ is the provider of the covenant, not the Law!

God is the controller of time and eternity, but to say that the Holy Spirit will be removed from the earth during this time is certainly reading a lot into 2 Thessalonians, and other passages on this subject, that just isn't there. The Holy Spirit will certainly lift restraint from the Antichrist, but will not let him out of His sight, for God is always in control of history and of its events.

One more thing we find is that the restrainer of verse 6 is explained as a "he" in verse 7. The Church is never described in Scripture as a "he." The Church is the *bride* of Christ, not a "he." This, too, tells us that the restrainer is not the Church.

One has to ask, what is Paul's message here? What is he trying to tell the Thessalonians? The popular teaching tells us that Paul is rebuking the Thessalonians, because they believed that they were in the Tribulation already. Further, they contend that Paul had previously taught that the Church would not go through the tribulation. Now, Paul had written to the Thessalonians previously in 1 Thessalonians, and indeed he had spoken of the Second Coming and of the Rapture, but what had he taught concerning these events? The argument says that he taught a rapture prior to the Tribulation, but if that's the case, one has to ask: why did the Thessalonians believe that they were in the Tribulation? Also, it should be noted that there's no evidence that he taught this.

It would be easier to understand how the Thessalonians might have forgotten what Paul had taught them concerning the Antichrist. They might have forgotten that the Antichrist must be revealed before the Lord comes. But to think that they had believed the exact opposite of the teaching that Paul was supposed to have given them means that they had disbelieved or rejected Paul's teaching. If this were the case, you'd have thought that Paul's rebuke would have been much more stern. However, his message was: "Let no man deceive you by any means: for that day shall not come except there come a falling away first and that man of sin be revealed." He seems to be saying tribulation will always be with us, but don't forget that there are signs that will tell us of the Great Tribulation. The fact is that these Christians were looking for the Great Tribulation, and Paul didn't rebuke them for that. He instead told them to remember the one great sign, the same sign that the Lord had spoken of in the Mount Olivet discourse of Matthew 24, and the same sign that Daniel had spoken of in Daniel 11. The Antichrist would be the major sign.

I might add that there is some possible scriptural evidence that Michael the archangel could be the instrument that the Holy Spirit uses to restrain the Lawless one. Marvin Rosenthal makes a strong case for this as fact on page 257 of his book, *The Pre-Wrath Rapture of the Church.* [4]

Now, let me set the record straight. Though it's true that many will grow weak and fall away, it's also true, according to Scripture, that many in the end time will grow stronger. The saints of Revelation will not be powerless to resist Satan. They will overcome him with the blood of the Lamb and with the word of their testimony. Therefore I don't believe that a weakened Church will allow the Antichrist to rise to power, nor do I see from the teaching of Scripture that a raptured Church will be the instrument used to bring this about. In 2 Thessalonians, the disappearance of the Church becomes an issue only because man has made it an issue. Read this epistle and you will see that there is most certainly a clear case presented which supports the Rapture and Revelation (the coming of the Lord to this earth) as being one event. We have also seen this elsewhere in Scripture. Here there is no mention of the Church being removed before our Lord's return to this earth. What is true of this passage is that the Thessalonians believed that they were already in the Tribulation, and Paul was attempting to set them straight.

Things happened as we entered the decade of the 90s that most if not all believed impossible. The United States now seems to be more of an ally with Russia's leaders than a cautious restrainer of this once perceived enemy. The Iron Curtain has come down; the wall in Germany has come down. The world has unified against Iraq. There is at least the appearance that communism is dissolving before our very eyes. The new age certainly seems to be coming into its own. We may indeed be standing on the brink of something new, but something entirely different and certainly more dangerous than most suspect.

The New Ager looks for his christ by the year 2000. Are these things possible in our day? Are folks at higher levels really into this? An article in the June

18, 1990 *Time* magazine entitled "Gorby, the New Age Guru?" may seem insignificant to most readers, but if you put two and two together you may become concerned. In this article the writer acknowledges "frequent use" of "new age" terms by Mikhail Gorbachev. The article also acknowledges the similarity between new age "philosophy" and that of the former Soviet president. These philosophies are linked to the new world order. In his speech in California just before this article was published Gorbachev stated that "all mankind is entering a new age and world trends are beginning to obey new laws and logic."[5] Other world leaders, some of them "Christian," are also seeing our times differently. This quote is taken from the religious section of the Lynchburg, VA, city newspaper.

> NEW YORK (AP) "Jimmy Carter, an ex-president who keeps busy at good works and unofficial diplomacy, says chroniclers of events don't adequately recognize the influence of the religious factor. . . . he said he has 'developed a broader perspective' about religion, more open to faiths of others, recognizing a 'lot of commonality' among different historic religions. 'Almost all of them call for justice, peace, service, equality, some humility,' he said. 'And the finer aspects of our faith (Christianity) are expressed in those terms."[6]

We must ask: Is this time of great falling away near? We really don't know for sure, but listen to another New Age prophet who is sharing her thinking on its nearness.

> Humanity is considered to have moved forward to the point where the theories and ideals of the Mystery Teaching may soon be put into practice in the life of the community as a whole, because a sufficiently large number of people are now so

advanced as to make this possible. The ancient writings all claim that a Golden Age is indeed due to follow the death of the present Dark Age.

It seems unquestionable that a time has now arrived in history where an attempt to rebuild civilization will—and must be made. . . . Plans and hope for world reconstruction are now universal and permeate all strata of the community.[7]

It certainly appears that the New Age plan is coming together, and if it is, it's only because God is allowing it to occur because it's in His timing.

If all that the New Age says is even remotely possible, and if Satan is the potential motivating force, then what we are seeing from Scripture concerning these days is for the Christian. But if they are, many among us are still asleep. We need to awaken to the fact that Mystery Babylon will deceive the Church, and many will fall away. The Antichrist will use false religion even within the Church.

SIX

ARE THERE TWO STAGES TO THE SECOND COMING?

As an introduction to this section, I want you to think about the prophecies related to our Lord's first appearing. These are well-stated in many of the prophetic books of our day. Several writers have done an outstanding job of listing these clearly stated prophecies from Scripture. There are at least sixty such prophesies, all of which saw their fulfillment in the Lord Jesus, and which are confirmed in the New Testament.[1] Many of these prophecies were so clearly stated that men had to be blinded by Satan in order that they would not see them. This blindness was allowed by God as a punishment for their failure to repent. Israel was given a clear opportunity to repent following the Lord's resurrection, but because of her refusal to repent, the blindness remained.

The Scriptures nonetheless were clear, and many understood. It was clear when the Lord would come. Daniel's prophecy that He would be cut off pinpointed it to the very year. He would be a descendant of David (Jer. 23:5, Ps. 132:11), born of a virgin (Isa. 7:14), a worker of miracles (Isa. 35:5-6), come to His temple (Mal. 3:1), and many more. Yet, there are also clear statements of His death. He would be rejected by the Jews (Isa. 53:3), betrayed by a friend (Ps. 41:9), sold for thirty pieces of silver (Zech. 11:12), falsely accused (Ps. 35:11, 27:12), whipped (Isa. 53:5), rejected (Isa. 53:3), crucified (Ps. 22:16; Zech. 12:10), mocked on the cross (Ps. 22:6-8), His bones would not be broken (Ps. 34:20), His side would be pierced (Zech.12:10). Daniel had also stated that He would be cut off.

But even with all of this evidence, we can still excuse the Jews for misunderstanding these prophecies, because their focus was on the Kingdom, not the sacrificial Lamb. Remember, the Jews did not know that there would be a first and a second coming. They did not have the completed Word of God! But even so, God had told them in the Scriptures which they did have (the Old Testament) that there would be this cutting off (death) of the Messiah. We, however, have the completed Scripture. We say that we know from Scripture that His coming will be in two stages. OK! Now, let's prove it. Will the man with the scriptural proof please stand up.

Grant Jeffrey, in his book, *Armageddon: Appointment with Destiny*, asks, **"Why do some teach that the Church will go through the Tribulation?"** [2]

He then states, ". . . they have two problems or premises which force them to reject the teaching of this book . . . The first is an emotional one which contends that, since the Church has known persecution and tribulation throughout its two-thousand-year history, . . . it would somehow be *unfair* for the Church of the Western world to 'escape to Heaven scotfree' . . . (and) the failure to distinguish between God's plan for Israel and the Church, especially in that prophecy revealed by Christ in Matthew 24."[3] Remember, Mr. Jeffrey had explained that Matthew 24 records Christ explaining to "His Jewish disciples" indicators that would point to the return of our Lord as "their Jewish Messiah."

He then lists *"Five definite indications"* supporting

"the pre-tribulation Rapture": "*First, . . . from Revelation chapter 4-19 . . . there is not one mention of the church on the earth . . .* The Church is described during this period as participating in the Marriage Supper of the Lamb and at the 'bema' judgment seat before Christ in Heaven . . ." (No Scripture is given on either of these points.)

"*Second,* Revelation 4 tells us that when John was '**in the Spirit**' and was 'raptured' up to Heaven, and that he saw twenty-four elders with crowns on their heads.[4]

Third, . . . Matthew 24 describes the events of the Tribulation and focuses on Israel, *not* the Church. . . .

Fourth, . . . (1 Thessalonians 5:9) . . . the Church has *not* been appointed by God to the wrath of the Great Tribulation.

Fifth, . . . (and his last argument) one of the strongest proofs that the Rapture will precede the revealing of the man of lawlessness, the Antichrist, is found in 2 Thessalonians 2:1-9. . . ." [5]

Most of the Scriptures that Jeffrey used in the first four arguments were listed in the quote above. Additional Scriptures which he listed are as follows: Dan. 9:27; Rev.13:7; John 14:16-17; John 16:8-11; and 1 Thess. 1:10.[6] But, again, just as most pre-trib advocates, Jeffrey's focus is basically *theory* as it concerns the Second Coming. Although he does use a good deal of Scripture, a careful study of the Scriptures listed in these five arguments should in no way convince any one of us of a two-part coming.

It is not my purpose to put down Grant Jeffrey and others quoted in this book, who, like him, are studying the Word. The fact is that all of these theories are just that. There are no "clear Scriptures" (even though Mr. Jeffrey contends otherwise) which state that the Church will be in heaven during the Great Tribulation. Further, he gives us no indication who those are who support the post-tribulation position, yet admit that Jeffrey's statements hold up. The truth is that Mr. Jeffrey has done more to disprove the pre-trib rapture in his book than he's done to support it.

Again I ask: "Will the real holder of scriptural facts in support of a pre-trib Rapture please come forth?" If the Old Testament pointed out in great detail the two separate comings of our Lord, then the completed Scriptures also should confirm the two separate stages of the Second Coming. But this is not the case. As we continue to look at the scriptural evidence for this view, we have to wonder where evidence is presented in Scripture on the two stages of our Lord's Second Coming.

We can observe that the Second Coming is spoken of no less than 300 times within Scripture, and that most of these times it is referred to, it's understood as the *next* appearing of Christ. It's never referred to as an intermediate or third coming. There is no definite single passage in Scripture to explain this as two separate events. Yet, where did the doctrine come from?

Erickson, who had thoroughly researched the question through all of the witnesses states that "Pretribulationists generally concede that there is no complete statement of pretribulationism in the writings of the early fathers."[7]

He further concluded concerning later church history:

> In the early nineteenth century clear-cut pre-tribulationism arose in the views of John Nelson Darby (1800-1882), a member of the Plymouth Brethren movement...[whose] view expounded [one] much like that found in the early Church: a futuristic view of the coming of the Antichrist, who will inflict severe persecution upon the

Church during the great tribulation. According to this view Christ will return at the end of the tribulation to deliver His Church. Darby introduced a modification of this view: "Christ will come to rapture the Church before the Tribulation and before He comes in glory to establish the millennial kingdom."[8] (The question that must be asked is: from what source did Darby receive his modification?)

Dave MacPherson, in his book, *The Unbelievable Pre-Trib Origin*, thoroughly documents the history of events, from the actual inception of a two-part theory to its development as a doctrine. Its birth was given by Margaret Macdonald, who spoke forth its origin just prior to her involvement in the charismatic outbreak of the 1830s in Scotland. The message was received as a prophetic revelation, and was later picked up by Darby, who hid its origin, but propagated its message.[9] Darby did in fact visit Margaret Macdonald's home town, and after doing so renounced the happenings which were taking place there. INTERESTING!!

The actual recording of Miss Macdonald's involvement was discovered, after much travel and searching, by MacPherson in a book purchased from an Illinois bookstore. The book entitled *The Restoration of the Apostles and Prophets in the Catholic Apostolic Church* (1861), was authored by a contemporary of Miss Macdonald, a Dr. Robert Norton, M.D. Dr. Norton's book contained the following paragraph:

> Marvellous light was shed upon Scripture, and especially on the doctrine of the second Advent, by the revived spirit of prophecy. In the following account by Miss M. M——, of an evening during which the power of the Holy Ghost rested upon her for several successive hours, in mingled prophecy and vision, we have an instance; for here we first see the distinction between that final stage of the Lord's coming, when every eye

shall see Him, and His prior appearing in glory to
them that look for Him.[10]

Is it not interesting how God preserves certain
facts in history for those who seek the truth? Thanks
to Dave MacPherson we now know the truth. His book
also records that Edward Irving, who was also a part of
this same movement, was pronounced a heretic for
denying the deity of the Lord Jesus Christ.

Those who see a pre-trib rapture find a major
difference in our Lord's coming first as a thief for His
saints, and then later with His saints in the clouds.
These stages they say prove the two-part Second
Coming. Let's look at the distinction in these stages.
Scriptural arguments have been generated to support
two views of this theory based on the Lord coming as
a thief. What exactly do the Scriptures imply by this
term *thief*? Some believe that *thief* is used as a symbol
of judgement, so they relate this coming of the Lord
to His coming at the close or end of the age, for it is at
this time that He will come as Judge. Others see His
coming as a thief as a secret snatching away of the
Church. Both views have problems.

The second stage of the Second Coming is drawn
from the scriptural teaching that Christ will come in
the clouds. This is the event which is argued by others
in the movement as being His coming for the Church.
Here they say we are seen caught up to be with him in
the air (clouds). However, those who see the Rapture
occurring when He comes as a thief argue that this is
His final coming in the eastern sky where every eye will
behold Him. Here He comes with all of His saints and
sets His feet on the Mount of Olives. This would be a
fulfillment of the prophecy by the angels in Acts 1. The
angels stated that Christ would return in like manner
as he was taken up (in a cloud). Obviously, there is
confusion; this confusion is indicative of the fact that

both of these descriptions can be used interchangeably, thus can be representative of the same event. In other words, the two parts may possibly be one after all.

Why is there this confusion among theologians who in the end agree on the same pretribulational doctrine? The answer lies in the Scriptures. As stated before, depending on one's view, either event can point to the Rapture or to the final coming in judgment to set up the kingdom. Beyond the reasons already given above, the Scriptures lead us to see that both the coming of Christ as a thief and His coming in the clouds are occurring at the same time after the Tribulation. 2 Peter 3:10 says, "But the day of the Lord will come like a thief, and then the heavens will pass away with a loud noise." Remember, a day is as 1000 years to the Lord. The period to which Peter is referring is the Millennium, after which the earth will pass away, as Peter states. This passage is often used as a proof text to disprove the literal Millennium by amillennialists; yet, when this passage is seen through God's eyes with a literal understanding and relating it to other scripture, then it really isn't confusing at all.

Just when does the Lord come as a thief? If we look at Revelation 16:15–16, we see that Christ, while giving John the revelation, announces His coming as a thief just prior to the event known as the battle of Armageddon. This is obviously a reference to His coming to destroy the Antichrist and bring judgment upon those who have openly rejected Him. Yet, we should look at how this is seen by some advocates of the pre-tribulation position. Oliver Greene states the Lord's coming "as a thief" is His coming for the Church prior to Tribulation. He states:

> Why did the Holy Spirit compare the Rapture to a thief coming in the darkness of night? The answer is clear: Even a child knows what a thief

is, what he does, and how he does it. When Jesus
comes in the Rapture His coming will be unex-
pected by the world. Believers are looking for
Him, waiting for Him and praying for His soon
return; "but as it was in the days of Noah, so shall
it be in the days of the coming of the Son of
man."In Noah's day the people ate, they drank,
they bought, they sold, they married wives "and
knew not until the flood came and took them all
away." . . . When Jesus comes in the Rapture, He
will take the jewels (the born again ones), but He
will not be seen by unbelievers.[11]

This is the gist of Mr. Greene's argument. However, it has obvious errors. In Rev. 16, Christ comes as
a thief to begin His reign and to judge those unbelievers that Mr. Greene states will not see Him. Also, the
Lord Jesus used the illustration of Noah's day to depict
sudden judgment, while Greene uses it to teach a
rapture. The Lord spoke of two being in the field, "one
is taken and one is left," of two at the mill, "one is taken
and one is left." Yet, even though this is often used to
depict the Rapture, it actually speaks of judgment. His
coming as a thief will be to judge the world.

Walvoord and Zuck, who agree with Greene
doctrinally on the Rapture, disagree with him on his
interpretation of Noah's day. "'As it was in Noah's day,
so it will be before the glorious **coming of the Lord.
Two men will be in the field; one will be taken and the
other left. Two women will be grinding with a hand
mill; one will be taken and the other left.'** Analogous
to Noah's day, the individuals who will be 'taken' are
the wicked whom the Lord will take away in judgment
(cf. Luke 17:37). The individuals "left" are believers
who will be privileged to be on the earth to populate
the kingdom of Jesus Christ in physical bodies."[12]

Although Walvoord disagrees with Greene on
the analogy of Noah, he still agrees with him in the

Rapture itself. He also sees those believers who are left after the Rapture as being those who will populate the kingdom. Is he right? Consider Rev 20:4 to see if you agree that believers who come out of the Tribulation will in fact populate the coming kingdom. Does it look like those who Christ will rule over with a rod of iron (Rev.19-15), or does it instead sound like those who will reign with Christ (the Church)? Those who actually populate the kingdom will be ruled with a rod of iron by Christ, and will also be ruled by those who reign with Him (the Church).

The Lord is described not only as coming as a thief, but He will also come in the clouds. If we consider Rev. 1:7, here we see Him coming in the clouds, and every eye sees Him. We should also understand just what's happening—here on earth men are wailing because of His coming. The wailing must be because of His judgment in Rev.19:11. In Mark 13:26, we see the gathering of the elect as He comes in the clouds. In Mark 14:62, the Lord confirms that men will witness this coming. In these Scriptures we find a complete picture of Christ's return with His saints. The saints were taken up to be with Him at His coming, as Mark 13:26 records it. The post-tribulational position on the Rapture, would line up with the events as seen within these verses.

Now, we must ask: is His coming in the clouds in conflict with His coming as a thief? And what of other Scriptures on this event that show Him coming at the twinkling of an eye, at the sound of the last trumpet, announcing final judgment?

Oliver Greene includes a section in his book, *Bible Truth*, on the two stages of Christ's Second Coming. In it, he begins by quoting 1 Thessalonians 5:6, the passage having to do with the Lord's coming as a thief; and 1 Corinthians 15:51-58, where Paul speaks of the mystery of our being changed into immortality. He then makes the following observation: "These passages just quoted have reference to the Rapture, the first stage of the Second Coming of Jesus—the time when He will come for His saints."[14] He then refers to the second stage listing the following passages: Zech. 14:1-5; 2 Peter 3:10-14; Rev. 1:7; and Rev. 19:11-16. Mr. Greene now continues: "Now, if we allow the Holy Spirit to lead in the study of these verses, by comparing Scripture with Scripture we can readily see that the two *groups* of Scriptures quoted here do not relate to the same event. It is evident that the Second Coming of Jesus is definitely in two stages—the Rapture, and the Revelation." Mr. Greene explains: "So when Jesus comes the second time, in the first stage of His coming (the Rapture) He will bring with Him the spirits of the righteous who have departed this world, and at that time their bodies will be raised incorruptible. However, He will not at that time descend to the earth. He will come *in the clouds in the air* and will call the saints up to meet Him there."

Greene has shown where the Lord was to come for the Church as a thief, and where He would come both in the clouds and as a thief *with his saints*. And now Greene is also saying that He will rapture the Church in the clouds. Greene intermixes these two "different" events, yet he says that these two groups of Scriptures are unrelated. I suggest that you read all of these passages of Scripture, and then judge whether or not they are related.

When we consider that the Lord comes both suddenly as a thief in Revelation 19, and also in the clouds in Revelation 1:7, then we can see that the Scripture's teaching becomes clear. When we see His Second Coming as the Second Coming, and not as a third Coming, then confusion is avoided.

SEVEN

WHAT IS GOD'S DEFINITION OF THE CHURCH?

Here we'll take up perhaps the strongest argument in support of the Pre-tribulation rapture. The argument states that the Church doesn't appear in Revelation after the fourth chapter, and does not reappear until after the Tribulation is over. This indeed can be seen as strong evidence that the Church isn't here during the Great Tribulation. Indeed, it was the first of Jeffery's five "clear indicators" listed in chapter 6. But does the fact that the word "Church" doesn't appear mean that the Church isn't present? Can we build a doctrine on the absence of a word? The word "Church" appears seventy-nine times in the New Testament. "Churches" appears thirty-five times. Neither word appears in 2 Peter, 1 John, 2 John, or Jude. Neither word appears in Mark, Luke, or John. In other words, "church" or "churches" do not appear in a significant block of the New Testament. John, the writer of Revelation, didn't use the word "Church" in three of his other four writings. Why is all of this significant? The mere absence of the Church in a section of Scripture doesn't mean the absence of the body of believers. They were and still are today called by many different names: Christian, brethren, saint, little children, the elect lady, the Commonwealth of Israel, The Bride, the elect, and others. All these are used to denote believers.

Saints

The term used often for believers during the Tribulation is "saints." I discovered that the term "saint" is used sixty times in the New Testament and thirty-seven times in the Old Testament. In each case in the New Testament, it refers to believers in Christ. And I would suggest to you that the same is true of Old Testament saints—based on what we have seen and will see from Scripture. John didn't use the word *church* when describing believers. Instead, he used *elect lady* and *children* most often. He didn't use the term *saints* at all until Revelation. In Revelation he uses *saints* thirteen times and *brethren* four times.

Now, as I considered that *saints* was used most often in Revelation to describe believers, I felt it extremely important to explore the relationship of the Church and the saints. Hal Lindsay, in *The Late Great Planet Earth*, wrote:

> The word "saint" means someone who is set apart as God's possession. It is used to designate all who have believed in Christ as Savior. This word is used many times to refer to those who will accompany Christ at His return.[1]

I saw that Mr. Lindsay failed to consider that his definition doesn't support his position, for the saints are on earth during the Tribulation, and certainly they can't accompany Christ at His return unless they're raptured just prior to His return at the end of the Tribulation. What then does Hal Lindsay do with the saints of Revelation? He re-defines them. On page 99 he states:

It is logical to ask at this point, how is he going to
make war with the saints when they are gone
from the earth? "The saints" are the people who
are going to believe in Christ during this great
period of conflict. After the Christians are
gone . . .[2]

As we look at Ephesians, we find the apostle Paul
begins this important doctrinal book with a greeting
to the "saints . . . who are also faithful." Perhaps it
could be argued that Paul's intent was not to write to
the entire church, but just to the faithful within that
church; yet even if this dubious interpretation were
true, it would have no negative bearing on this subject.
If the saints in Ephesus are the faithful, so would be the
saints that are to be present during the Great Tribulation. We see them in many places within Revelation.
It's true that some of these saints are in heaven
(surrounding the throne). But many are on this earth
being persecuted for their faith. This gives strong
evidence that the Church is present on this planet
during the Great Tribulation.

In Ephesians 1, Paul makes it clear how we are
born into the Church. It's a supernatural birth which
involves the work of the Holy Spirit as He seals us. In
chapter two, Paul sets out to explain the mystery of the
building of the Church. He tells who we once were
"children of wrath" and who we now have become
"fellow citizens with the *saints*, members of the household of God."

Paul makes it clear in Ephesians 2:11-12a what we
were before we came to Christ. At that time we were
outside looking in on the promises of the covenants.
But, listen to what we now are:

But now in Christ Jesus you who were once far off
[Gentiles] have been brought near in the blood
of Christ. For He is our peace, who has made us

both one, and has broken down the dividing wall of hostility, by abolishing in His flesh the law of commandments and ordinances, that He might create in Himself one new man in place of the two, so making peace, and might reconcile us both to God in one body the cross, thereby bringing the hostility to an end. (Eph. 2:13-16)

In this passage the concept of one new man created from the saved Jewish saints and the saved Gentile saints is very clear.

The church–ekklesia

Robert Saucy, in his book on the Church, *The Church in God's Program*, begins his study by relating the Greek word for Church (*ekklesia*) to the Old Testament in order to find its meaning. He points out that *ekklesia* "was a term for the assembly of citizens summoned by the crier."[3] It occurred almost one hundred times within the Septuagent as the Hebrew word *qahal*. [4] This idea of the Church, then, appears more in the Old Testament than it does in the New. Had we been present in the synagogues of that day, we would have heard the word *church* read from the Scriptures on a regular basis. Saucy further points out that "it is often argued that *qahal* became a sort of technical term for Israel in the Old Testament, meaning the people of God."[5] It was used to denote "the congregation of Israel" in Micah 2-5; Numbers 16:3.[6] So we see that the actual term that is translated *church* (*ekklesia*) was related to Israel prior to the Lord's coming.[7]

Remember, if the Greek was the language of the day, and the Old Testament was the only Scripture in use, then it becomes quite obvious that the word *church* was already prevalent when the Lord Jesus made his statement concerning His building the Church. The rock upon which Jesus would build His church was the truth Peter stated in Matt. 16:16, "You are the Christ, the Son of the living God." The Church would encompass "whosoever will," including the Jews of the Old Testament. Now, this was really beginning to fit together. The truth that Peter had stated was the truth that Israel had been hoping for. Peter was seeing that Messiah was here. He is the Messiah of the Old Testament saint and of the New testament saint, and we certainly can't leave out the Tribulation saint.

Saucy confirmed this by showing that the Church means "the spiritual unity of all believers in Christ."[8] Certainly if the Lord took Israel with Him from the grave, then they are part of the body of Christ as God intended it. This is exactly what the Scriptures teach that He did. For in establishing His Church, the Lord also led a host of "captivity captive," having stormed the very gates of hell itself. His purpose was to release those awaiting His arrival in paradise (Eph. 4:8-9; 1 Pet. 4:6). Those had to be the Old Testament Jewish saints. Remember that the Lord had said to the thief crucified next to Him, "This day shalt thou be with me in Paradise." So the Lord entered Paradise and released the Church of the Old Testament, leading these from captivity into the glory of heaven. This event was the beginning of the Church headed by Messiah.

God is not trying to teach us a pre-trib rapture by leaving the word *ekklesia* or *church* out of Revelation 4–19.

The elect

Another important and related Scripture needs to be explored here. In Rom. 11:7, Paul uses a different term for the Church. Here he uses the word *elect*, but it's how he uses it that's important. If you will remember, the Lord in His discourse on the Tribulation said, "For then there will be great tribulation . . . but for the sake of the elect, those days will be shortened" (Matt. 24: 21-22).[9]

Paul says in Rom. 11:7, "What then? Israel has not obtained what it seeks; but the elect have obtained it, and the rest were hardened." The first thing that I want you to see from this verse is that Israel the nation is not the elect spoken of in this passage, even though Paul is teaching here on the restoration of Israel at the end of the age. The (elect) remnant has now continued on into the Church. It, in fact, never left the Church, the *qahal* (Gk. *ekklesia*), of Israel. According to this passage of Scripture, the rest of Israel was hardened. Paul is speaking about Jews who have gone on into the New Covenant. He even speaks of the grafting in of the Gentiles into the New Covenant (the olive tree). Now these Gentiles have become a part of this same remnant, the *qahal*, the Church. To Timothy he makes a statement which confirms that the elect, when saved, will be in Christ: "Therefore I endure everything for the sake of the elect, that they also may obtain salvation in Christ Jesus with its eternal glory."[10] Here Paul speaks of those elect who are still in Israel, and who have not yet been saved.

The elect then represents both the Jewish remnant inside the Church, and the Jewish nation outside of the Church who are yet to be saved. If the elect became part of those who are in Christ, is the Church, then, part of the elect that the Lord spoke of in Matthew 24? Again, the answer here has to be yes, for even though the Church is made up of Jews and Gentiles, it's still the recipient of that which Israel failed to obtain. This New Covenant is what Israel seeks after. We're a part of God's elect.

You will recall that I had said that some are

teaching that these elect are those who are saved out of the Great Tribulation. (Again, just let me point out that there is no Scripture offered to support this theory, although some are very dogmatic in their teaching of it.) Grant Jeffrey is one such proponent of this position. In his book he says:

> These "elect" are the people who become believers during the Great Tribulation of three and a half years. This gathering together is not the Rapture. This gathering of the tribulation believers takes place at the end of the Tribulation, whereas the Rapture of the Church occurs sometime prior to the beginning of the Great Tribulation when Antichrist sets himself up as "God" in the temple.[11]

I will let you be the judge of whether or not this position lines up with what we just viewed from Scripture.

As I continued my search for the relationship between the saints of Revelation and the Church, I had to return to Romans, where the destiny of Israel is fully discussed in chapter 11. I found that not only does the Holy Spirit reveal the destiny of Israel, but He also reveals the time that this plan will come about. There is a mystery revealed here in verse 25 involving the Gentiles. According to this verse, Israel will be saved when the full number of the Gentiles have come in. Again, she will be saved just as you and I are saved—by accepting her Messiah. More evidence is provided when we examine just to whom the book of Romans was written. We would assume it to be the church at Rome; however, it too is addressed to "all God's beloved in Rome who are called to be saints". The issue is not that the letter is not addressed to the church—it is! The issue is how the church is addressed—those who are called to be saints. Again, we're seeing the use of the word *saints* to describe what has come to mean the Church to us.

Now the events of Revelation take on more significance. Tribulation saints are called to an endurance, for this is going to be a time of testing. Endurance calls for faith; faith is the shield against our enemy's onslaughts. Remember the Lord had said in Matthew 24 that "many will fall away" during this time of Great Tribulation, "but he who endures to the end will be saved." The times of the Gentiles will end with a regeneration of Israel, and just as there were Jews who led the way for the Gentiles at the time of Christ's first appearing, the Christian (you and I) will lead the way for the Jew's redemption. And that group of believers includes the saints, the Church, the elect.

EIGHT

IS THE RETURN OF CHRIST IMMINENT?

"Watch therefore—for you do not know when the master of the house will come, in the evening, or at midnight, or at cockcrow, or in the morning—lest he come suddenly and find you asleep. And what I say to you I say to all: Watch" (Mark 13:35-36).

Let me begin by stating that in fact at some point in history the return of the Lord will become imminent. At some future time, all prophecy will become fulfilled. To those Christians who see these events, His coming will be imminent! Yet, there is another hurdle that has to be explored to see if literal interpretation will stand the test of consistency. The popular teaching of our day is that the Church has always expected the imminent return of Christ. The teaching calls for a return which could have occurred at any moment, and argues that this message was taught by the early Church, otherwise they would have been looking for the Tribulation rather than the coming of the Lord.

First. In order for this argument to be valid, it must have been so for all generations since the very earliest times of the Church. Thus all prophecy concerning the Second Coming must have been fulfilled during the times of the first-generation church.

Second. The early Church is said to have been looking for Christ's return at any moment. It's argued that this fact proves the doctrine of a pre-trib rapture.

Third. We have the problem of defining exactly when the Lord's return became imminent during the first century. Was it after Pentecost, or after the Scripture was complete? Or was it later, and if so, why? This, as I viewed it, was one of those doctrines that we are asked to accept on faith. Unfortunately, those who ask us to do so don't seem to understand what they ask. "Faith," according to God's Word, "cometh by hearing, and hearing by the Word of God" (Rom. 10:17). I was again seeking scriptural support for this part of the doctrine.

In order to determine the scriptural validity of the first argument, I had to look at prophecy and its fulfillment. We'll start here in the same manner with the understanding that all prophecy has to be fulfilled in order for Christ to return. Any prophecy that could be dated would need to have seven years deducted from it, because the Lord is to return seven years early, if the pre-tribers are correct. Next, I had to look for those prophecies which are to be fulfilled within the times of the New Testament Church. Here I only needed to go as far as prophecy concerning Israel's rebirth as a nation in order to answer my question. Jesus had said that when we see the signs spoken of in Matthew chapter 24, we should lift up our heads, for our "redemption draweth nigh." One of the signs was the budding of the fig tree, which many see representing the rebirth of the nation Israel. This sign not only was not fulfilled within the first generation following Christ, neither was it fulfilled within any generation since that time up until our own. This prophecy has now come to pass within our day. However I still had a nagging question—could this prophecy have been fulfilled at any time in church history?

I decided to explore this further. Daniel's seventy weeks seemed to me to be a good place to start. According to Daniel, seventy weeks were to come to pass in order to fulfill all Daniel's prophecy. Daniel was taught by the Lord specifically about the empires which would be in power until the establishment of the messianic kingdom (Daniel 7:27). He was shown how each kingdom would unfold right up until the end, when the Messiah would set up His kingdom. This is, of course, the millennial kingdom for which you and I are waiting. He would set it up by crushing the Antichrist.

Daniel saw the number of weeks until the coming of Messiah (seven and sixty-two weeks from the going forth of the decree to rebuild Jerusalem). Most will equate Daniel's 70th week (that is, the week itself), with the seven years of tribulation recorded in Revelation. They see it as a literal seven years in duration, unless it would be cut short by the Lord's return.

The question of course becomes whether or not the Lord could have returned immediately after the establishment of the New Covenant at Pentecost? NO! If you would consider that according to God's revelation to Daniel, there were four beasts, each representing an empire, which would rule the earth over the course of Gentile history. The final of these four beasts was the Roman Empire. This beast would bring forth ten kingdoms (Dan. 7:24), and after these ten kingdoms yet another kingdom would appear. This last kingdom is the kingdom of the Antichrist. This kingdom will be destroyed by the Messiah. Rome was still in power after the destruction of Jerusalem in A.D. 70. In the year A.D. 135, when Rome crushed the last uprising of the Jews, there were still no ten kingdoms. Yet ten kingdoms had to arise before the establishment of the kingdom of the Antichrist. Three of these ten would be put down at the setting up of Antichrist's kingdom (Dan. 7:24-25).

Simple math tells us that Israel could not have been dealt with as a nation in her final week, as the Dispensationalists understand that week, until many years after Rome would give birth to these kingdoms. Since the Rapture, according to the pre-trib belief, would occur 7 years prior to the Lord's return to crush the Antichrist, and since his kingdom is after the rise of ten kings that proceed from Rome, then this argument of an imminent return is not mathematically acceptable until all of this is fulfilled. Based on God's own Word, this is false.

Dave Hunt agrees with the argument put forth above with regard to the Second Coming of the Lord to establish His kingdom. He says ". . . that the second coming cannot occur until five related events have taken place first. . . ."[1]

Hunt states that one of these five events is the revival of the Roman Empire. And although we agree with Dave Hunt here, Hunt then argues that the return of Christ has always been "imminent."[2] His position is illogical if he believes that the timing of the Second Coming has never been ripe until now, and that the Rapture must occur seven years prior to the actual earthly return of the Lord. He, in fact, believes both.[3] How can he argue both ways?

But this is not all. Hunt also argues that the reason the Rapture is imminent is this: "To be caught up at the Rapture to meet Christ in the air and to be taken to heaven without experiencing physical death is the great hope of the Christian."[4] He then quotes Titus 2:13: "Looking for the blessed hope, and the glorious appearing of the great God and our Savior Jesus Christ." All Christians have this blessed hope of our Lord's appearing. We don't have to be the last generation in order to hold to this hope. And although this hope will be fulfilled in the Rapture, which is at the appearing of our Lord in glory, the timing of this appearing has nothing to do with our holding to this hope!

There have been some other interesting, but emotional, theories put forth regarding imminence. For instance, Grant Jeffrey states that "During the last two hundred years, this belief in the imminent return of Christ for His Church has been a strong motivating factor to encourage Christian missions . . ."[5] Based on this quote, it is certainly interesting that the belief in the imminent return has in Jeffrey's mind been the motivating influence on the missions work of our day. Our motivation is to be obedient, not the imminence of our Lord's return! If imminence is involved at all, it's in the possibility of an early demise or imminent death of those around us without the truth. This should be our motivation from imminence.

There is an irony to Mr. Jeffrey's argument, for he obviously believes in the imminent return of our Lord, and supports it. There is an inconsistency in his whole stand, however. If we consider his teaching that the rebirth of Israel in May of 1948 was a prophesied event right out of the Old Testament, then we must conclude that Christ could not have possibly come to rapture the Church as he teaches.[6]

Think about what Jeffrey and Hunt have failed to see in this argument. Remember, they see a rapture which could have occurred back in the first century; yet, Jeffrey says that a lost Israel would have remained unsaved until 1948, had the Rapture occurred before our time. Hunt basically says the same thing, because he argues that our time is the time for the Second Coming. There are two problems here. First, biblical prophecy cannot be wrong—the ten nations must first rise out of Rome. Second, Israel's salvation as a nation is directly tied to the completion of the salvation of the Gentiles. The Apostle Paul put it this way:

". . . a hardening has come upon part of Israel, until the full number of the Gentiles come in, and so all Israel will be saved . . . " (Rom.11:25-27a.). This passage of Scripture gives definite confirmation that Israel's future salvation is linked to the final salvation of the Gentile convert in this age. Paul states that once the final Gentile is saved, Israel will then be saved as a nation. Since this must occur in the fullness of time, it precludes any premature rapture or coming of the Lord.

Now, this alone would indicate that the time of Christ's return could not have been imminent, at least prior to our day. There are some who would say that even though the Lord's coming was not imminent before, that it certainly could be today. They might argue that now all prophecy has been fulfilled. This, I think, will clearly be seen as a weak argument in light of scriptural evidence. For instance, the Antichrist is the greatest sign of the Lord's coming. Also, in Acts 3:19, Peter said the Jews must repent that "He may send the Christ appointed for you." He then went on to explain that heaven had received him (Christ) "until the time for establishing all that God spoke by the mouth of his holy prophets from of old." There are two important truths brought out here. One we have already mentioned—all prophecy must be fulfilled before Christ will return. But what about Israel's repentance spoken of in this verse? If you read the context, you'll see what Peter said. The second thing is that God is waiting for the repentance of Israel. This He intends to bring about in a day which will begin with Armageddon. Here the Holy Spirit is confirming the word of God to the Jew, and advising them when Messiah will come.

It could, of course, be argued here that Peter was

simply telling the Jews when Christ would come to them, and that this doesn't necessarily imply that His coming for the Church is the same event. However, Peter was inviting these Jews to repent and accept Christ. They would therefore become part of the Church—would they not?

If this is not convincing enough evidence to refute imminence before the signs are complete, then let's take a look at the greatest New Testament prophet, the Lord Jesus Himself.

First. Our Lord stated that the gospel would be preached to all of the world, and then will the end come (not yet fulfilled), and this will not be fulfilled until during the tribulation (Rev.14:6 KJV).

Second. The temple and the buildings surrounding the Temple would be destroyed. He had said that not one stone would be left upon another (fulfilled in A.D. 70). It appears that in A.D. 70 the Temple had been completely destroyed. Yet many consider this prophecy incomplete, since the Wailing Wall still stands, constructed from the very stones of the Temple itself.

Third. Jerusalem would be trodden down by the Gentiles until the times of the Gentiles is complete (not yet complete). Since the Gentile nations today are the primary recipients of the New Covenant, this is an extremely important prophecy.

Fourth. Israel must be a nation (complete).

Fifth. The Tribulation must come (Matt. 24: 29–31). "Immediately after the Tribulation . . . will appear the sign of the Son of Man in heaven." In Mark's gospel this gathering is said to be "from the ends of heaven to the ends of earth" (Mark 13:24-27).

Some would say, "But we are not to look for the Tribulation, but for the blessed hope, the coming of the Lord." This is true, but it doesn't change the fact that the Great Tribulation will precede that glorious event, and will in fact be one of the major signs of that event. At some point after the coming of the Anti-christ, the Lord's coming will become imminent; and since this time will be cut short, no man will know the day or the hour.

If we might divert ourselves for just a moment and consider this fact: the disciples had asked the Lord Jesus to explain His coming in Matthew 24:3. In that question, they wanted to know the sign of the Lord's coming and of the close of the age. In answering this question, the Lord gave certain signs. The disciples had asked for signs, so He gave them signs (seems reasonable). Notice the signs (v. 9–14). After listing the signs appear the words, "and the end will come." The Lord answered the apostles' question with signs just as they had asked Him to do.

Paul teaches the Thessalonians about God's plan in 2 Thess. 1:5–10. In verse 5, he says we are made worthy by our suffering. In verse 6, he says the Lord will repay those who afflict us. Then Paul makes a startling announcement. He says God will grant us rest with the apostles "*when* the Lord Jesus is *revealed* from heaven *with* his mighty angels in flaming fire." Thus our rest will come with the coming of the Lord in what the pre-tribulation advocate says is the "revelation" of Christ.[7] Do you see this? Our rest is not to begin seven years prior to His coming with the mighty angels, but at that very moment. Not only did Paul not teach the Rapture before the Tribulation, but he taught it as being after the Tribulation. No wonder the Thessalonians were looking for the Tribulation.

Paul further states that this "punishment of eternal destruction" will come "when he comes on that day to be glorified in his saints." That is the day that we will see Him as He is; not prior to the Tribulation but, after it. On that day He will be glorified, and the sons of God will be revealed. The Tribulation is perhaps the most important sign of His coming, yet when writing on this passage in 2 Thess. 1:5–10, Walvoord and Zuck ignore this truth as they conclude: "It is clear that Paul had taught them a pre-tribulational rapture. Their confusion arose because they could not distinguish their present troubles from those of the day of the Lord."[8] The scriptural proof offered by these knowledgeable scholars for this dogmatic position is taken from 1 Thess. 1:10. If you read this passage in light of what has already been studied, you will find no such proof upon which to base such a statement. If we consider that the Thessalonians thought that they were in the Tribulation as Walvoord and Zuck teach, then Paul certainly missed the boat in trying to clear up their confusion. It would seem to me that if I were commissioned by the Holy Spirit to clear up the peoples' understanding of a rapture prior to the Tribulation, then I would have said: "The Lord Jesus is coming back for you before the Great Tribulation, and then in seven years you will receive your rest. Don't you remember that I told you this when I was with you." But Paul says: God's rest will come to you when "the Lord Jesus is revealed from heaven with his mighty angels in flaming fire." You know—the time when "vengeance is inflicted upon those who do not know God." In other words, the time of God's WRATH. Folks, Paul wasn't a Scripture-twister; he in fact condemned this. So if he said what they say he said, why can't we see where he just says it? This passage teaches that Christ will give us rest at His coming, when He is revealed.

What *did* Paul say? What did Paul mean by "rest"? Rest from what? Certainly we'll not need rest from seven years spent with the Lord in our glorified bodies. These bodies are not to need rest. Rest from what? Rest from the Marriage Supper of the Lamb? We can only conclude that the rest Paul is speaking of here is the rest from the tribulations of this life. Paul

explains these persecutions in the earlier verses outlined there.

The fact is that there was not even one word
spoken to imply that the Church would be raptured
prior to the Great Tribulation. He taught on the
Rapture! No question there will be one. He taught on
the signs that would precede the Rapture; the Antichrist must first be revealed. He also taught that we are
not appointed for wrath, and it certainly seems clear
that he taught that we would be raptured at the end of
the Tribulation.

God is not the author of confusion. Paul, as
God's instrument, explains this time as the time of the
"last trumpet." It also seems that he explained just
what he had meant by God's wrath when he explained
Christ's coming to inflict vengeance and eternal destruction. In my humble opinion, these Thessalonians
had no problem understanding what Paul had told
them. Remember this entire issue just might be plain,
rather than confusing.

Erickson's conclusion about the imminence issue is that some misconstrue the lack of data concerning the number, nature, and duration of intervening
events as implying immediacy. He goes on to add:
"Further it appears that when the 'watch' and the 'you
do not know the time' passages were written they
could not possibly have meant an any-moment imminency. For one thing, Jesus indicated to the early
disciples that His coming would be delayed for some
time."[9] References he uses to support this are Matt.
5:5, Luke 19:11-27, and Matt. 25:19. If you read these
passages, you will find that he is absolutely correct. A
most convincing argument in Scripture is where the
Lord had told Peter by what means he must die.[10] We
have to ask ourselves: Does this sound as if the Lord
intended to teach an imminent return in the days of
the penning of the gospel?

We have one other item to consider to either strengthen or weaken our argument on imminency. The early Church is said to have been looking for Christ's return at any moment. Does this explain when His coming becomes imminent? The promise of His coming is an integral part of the gospel message itself. But did the Lord ever say that He might come at any moment? For that matter did the apostles ever say that he might come at any moment? The Lord's emphasis was on watchfulness and not so much for His coming as for the signs of His coming. The apostle's warning concerned the spirituality of the saints. The issue was being in tune with and knowing the will of God. Certainly there are passages that one could point to that would indicate imminency, but each of these relate to knowing the signs, or at the very least not missing the signs. The signs are the key to watchfulness and the fact that the true saint of God will not be caught unawares. God will enlighten those who are awake and doing the will of the Father. He will enlighten them to know the times and the seasons, when those times actually arrive.

One of the things that has always puzzled me is the fact that our Lord had testified to ignorance when explaining the timing of these events. Yet, the apostle Paul wrote:

> But as to the times and seasons, brethren, you have no need to have anything written to you. For you yourselves know well that that day of the Lord will come like a thief in the night. When people say, "There is peace and security, then sudden destruction will come upon them as travail comes upon a women with child, and there will be no escape. But you are not in darkness, brethren, for that day to surprise you like a thief." (1 Thess. 5:1-4)

Have you ever thought why the apostle seemed to give greater wisdom and understanding to the Church at Thessalonica than God the Father had given to the Son?

Let's consider some of the facts surrounding all of this. Paul had obviously been to Thessalonica and taught on this subject. We know also that he was writing to correct an error related to the times and seasons of Christ's Second Coming. I also believe that all the apostles taught the signs of the Lord's coming, and these were most assuredly shared with the Thessalonians. It would be the signs that would point to the times and seasons. We can state further that the teaching that had confronted them had come from another source. And if this is the case, we can probably conclude that that source would have been a prophecy, for we know that prophecy was occurring in the Church. Was Paul not saying, "You foolish children, you have been given the signs of the Lord's coming, and you possess the Holy Spirit who will shed light on this matter when needed; (do not quench the Spirit, do not despise prophesying), but be sure that the prophecy is correct. Now, wake up and get back to work. The signs are not yet right. What you heard by the mouth of some prophet concerning the Lord's coming is not true, and you should know that! Wake up and examine the signs that have already been given you! Pay special attention to the sign of Antichrist!" This is the best reason, in light of Scripture, that Paul was upset with them for quitting prematurely.

NINE

WHAT IS THE MEANING OF REVELATION 3:10?

> Because you have kept my word of patient endurance, I will keep you from the hour of trial which is coming on the whole world, to try those who dwell upon the earth. (Rev. 3:10)

Discussion surrounding this verse revolves around the identity of the churches of Revelation 2 and 3 and the meaning of to "keep you from . . ." According to many theologians, each church in Revelation 3 represents a specific period of time in Church history (a dispensation) from the beginning to the end of the Church age, with the Laodicean church being the church present on earth during the time leading up to the Tribulation. She, of course, is represented as an apostate church. Her salvation is questionable.

If this is all true, we must ask why she was not also given the promise to be kept from this hour? One possible answer is that our understanding is wrong. The pre-trib dispensationalist seems to imply that the Laodicean church is totally lost, and therefore left to endure the Tribulation, while Philadelphia represents the saved church, and therefore there are no lost among them. In this view all of this church will be raptured, while all of the Laodiceans will be left to endure the Tribulation.

I again had some questions. First, if the Laodiceans represent an apostate non-church, why are they called a church age? Second, if they are the apostate church that brings in mystery Babylon, and have been totally rejected by Christ in the Rapture, why are they promised to sit with Christ on His throne? It would seem from Hebrews 10:26–31 that apostates are not allowed back into the church. Yet, the Lord says to the Laodiceans, "He who conquers, I will grant him to sit with me on my throne, as I myself conquered and sat down with my Father on his throne" (Rev.3:21).

Erickson, when writing on Rev. 3:10, states the following:

> A passage that has been the object of a great deal of scrutiny and controversy is Revelation 3:10: "Because you have kept my word of patient endurance, I will keep *(mpe'w)* you from *(ek)* the hour of trial which is coming on the whole world, to try those who dwell upon the earth"[1] The interpretation of this verse turns upon the significance of the preposition *ek*. Post-tribulationists argue basically that the primary sense of *ek*, "emergence from within," refutes the pre-tribulational interpretation of the verse. For the church to emerge from within the hour of testing, it must have been present in the testing. . . . John uses *ek* approximately 336 times, far more than any other New Testament writer. In every case the idea of emergence or origin is the meaning most suitable to the context. The Johannine usage of the word, then, appears to be well-established. . . . The same emphasis appears in Revelation 7:14, where the saints come "out of *ek* the great tribulation." The important question, said Gundry, is "why John did not use *arro* in Revelation 3:10, which would at least *permit* a pre-tribulational interpretation, or why he did not use a preposition that would *require* this

interpretation . . ."[2] The final issue in Revelation 3:10 is the meaning of the verb *rnpe'w*. When a situation of danger is in view, *rnpe'w* means to "guard." Danger is implicit in the idea of guarding. If the church is in heaven at this time, however, as pre-tribulationalism teaches, then what can be the danger that requires God's protecting hand upon her?[3]

Erickson confirms the importance of these two words as he elaborates on their usage in John 17:15.[4] Here they are used together when Jesus prays "that thou shouldst keep *(rnpe'w)* them from *(ek)* the evil one." The Lord's meaning in John 17 was to keep Christians from temptation and trials hurled against them from Satan. There is no reason to believe that the Lord's use of the exact same words is coincidental, and that they would not have the same connotation. But this is really not the issue. Philadelphia could be promised to be kept from ever seeing this day, and still it would not effect the Rapture issue.

Let me explain why I say this. First, if each church represents a dispensation within the church age, then there could be no imminent return for the first six church ages. By saying this I'm not supporting the Dispensational teaching on the seven churches, but merely pointing out the illogical argument within pre-tribulationism.

The real issue is deeper. This problem-laden-teaching seems to divert our attention from the actual truth we seek by focusing our attention to Revelation 3:10, causing us to ignore what the Lord is saying to the other churches in Asia. As we consider what these messages are saying, the idea of each church representing a different period in church history just doesn't add up. Sardis is said to represent the age just prior to Philadelphia. We, of course, are to be living in the Philadelphia age (according to the pre-trib doctrine), but we can see that Sardis was warned of Christ's coming as a thief (a warning that promised judgment for all except those who conquered). This warning is reasserted in Revelation after the events of the Tribulation are over, and as an announcement of the battle known as Armageddon.

But, going back even further to the third church, Thyatira, we see another warning. Here we see a definite picture of the church of the last days. Some in this church are practicing immorality with Jezebel. They are looking into the teaching that the Lord calls "the deep things of Satan." As a result they will be thrown into Great Tribulation (Rev. 2:22). I believe that we are seeing this satanic deception today as the Church is playing more and more with the New Age philosophy. The Lord will then allow the churches who are on earth at that time to know that Jesus is He who "searches the mind and heart," as He "rewards" those who "keep His works until the end" (Rev. 2:23). The implication here is that there will be a falling away, just as Jesus had warned in Matthew 24.

So again the point is that, while we are diverted to the message to Philadelphia and Revelation 3:10, we completely miss these other messages which warn the Church against involvement in sin leading us into the Tribulation. In fact, even if Philadelphia were to have completely disappeared off the scene, this would not change the teaching concerning the Rapture, because the Lord tells us in these messages that the Church will see this Great Tribulation. He even used the same Greek words used in Matthew 24:21 when speaking to Thyatira. So the real issue is: why are we being diverted, when Scripture is warning us that a portion of today's end time Church is in bed with the New Age false religious system that will be destroyed in the end. The warnings to the churches state that you and I need to be identified with the faithful saints of the Church who are told to hold on until the end.

TEN

GOD'S PLAN VERSUS THE CONFUSION

Scriptural answers to confusing issues

Reformed theology says that we are already in the Millennium. Christ is ruling through the Church. The Millennium is not a literal 1000 years, but now has extended for almost 2000 years. Most dispensationalists say that God has two peoples. They argue that the Church's inheritance is different than that of the Jew or Israel. The dispensationalists, who claim to be more literal, make a distinction between the kingdom of heaven and the kingdom of God. A raptured Church is seen first as being judged before the Lord Jesus, and then during the Tribulation we see the long awaited Marriage Feast of the Lamb. Meanwhile, the time of Jacob's trouble is taking place here on the earth. Let's break this down and consider the points, one at a time.

First, they say that the kingdom of the Church is a heavenly kingdom. We are seen in Scripture as seated at the right hand of Christ, and somehow we will mystically remain there during the Millennium. The promise to Israel at the same time is a promise of land and possessions. The contention here is that we will rule with Christ during the Millennium, and that we will rule at that time over the nation Israel and over the Tribulation saints, who will constitute the Gentile nations. The Scriptures do teach that we will reign with Christ, and that we will judge angels; but nowhere does it tell us that we will rule over Israel. This is mere speculation. What the Scriptures do tell us is that Christ will rule the nations with a rod of iron during the Millennium. Further, the nations are compared in Matthew to sheep on the right hand and goats on the left. Now just who are the nations represented by sheep? We are told by many of today's teachers that they are those who have come out of the Tribulation, having accepted the Lord Jesus. According to what is written in Scripture, they seem to be nations who have given refuge to the saints, who during the Tribulation will be able to neither buy nor sell. The Lord says that they have cared for His brethren. And this judgment of the nations is based on their good works or good deeds toward the brethren.

Christ's kingdom—of this earth, or a heavenly kingdom?

Some would tell us that there is no literal earthly kingdom. Others tell us that there are two kingdoms— one a heavenly kingdom, and the other an earthly kingdom. But the truth is that God's kingdom is one kingdom fulfilling both roles.

In John 18:33–37, the Lord Jesus answers a question from Pilate concerning the kingdom with these words: "My kingdom is not of this world." We could conclude from this, as many already have, that there will be no earthly reign of Christ. But to con-clude this would mean that everything else that the Lord states in Scripture concerning an earthly reign is null and void. What then did the Lord mean by "not of this world?"

If you will recall from the study on Rev. 3:10, we looked at the meaning of the words used by John. Ironically, again we have the same Greek wording used here that was used in John 17 within the Lord's prayer (*ek tov* —translated "out of the" world). The best translation of this statement then would be, "my kingdom is not out of this world or is not from this world." Any kingdom which arises out of this world will be crushed in the end by the eternal kingdom which Christ will set up. The Lord went on to say, "If my kingdom were *out of* this world, my servants would fight that I might not be turned over to the Jews." Jesus was not dependent on the world, on the power provided from the world, to establish His kingdom. His kingdom is according to the divine, eternal plan of Almighty God. And His kingdom will come in God's own timing.

"And in the days of those kings the God of heaven will set up a kingdom which shall never be destroyed, nor shall its sovereignty be left to another people. It shall break in pieces all these kingdoms and bring them to an end, and it shall stand forever" (Dan.2:44).

Our Lord's statement to Pilate was in perfect harmony with His plan to die for the sins of mankind, and then to build His Church from among those who would believe in Him and seek for His truth. But there is one other confusing point surrounding the kingdom. There are those who say that a conflict exists in Jesus teaching that can only be resolved by a two-part coming of the Lord. Our Lord had said in John 14 that He was going to prepare a place for us, that we could be with Him when He comes again. Dave Hunt has this to say concerning this passage:

"Some suggest that Christ catches up the Church to meet Him in the air, then beings her immediately back to earth with Him to rescue Israel and destroy her enemies. That hardly seems a fulfillment of His promise to take His own to His father's house—nor is it the way a bridegroom would treat his bride."[1]

The question is this—does this promise make it necessary for us to spend a period of time in heaven prior to the Second Coming of the Lord to establish the Millennium? In other words, do we have to receive this promise before we reign with the Lord? Besides, there is really nothing to suggest our returning doesn't happen. Other Scriptures plainly tell us of our glorious return with our Bridegroom.

Perhaps an illustration would help. Suppose an Israeli bridegroom were to say to his American bride, "I must go back to Israel and prepare a room for you in my father's house, and then I will come to take you to be with me forever!" Now, if two days or two months later he says to his American bride, "We will spend 1000 days in America when I return for you, does this second statement contradict that promise? The answer is no. This is exactly the method of the Lord's communication to us in Scripture—line upon line, precept upon precept, here a little there a little!

The Judgement of Israel and the saints

What is God's plan to bring Israel to repentance? The book of Revelation was given its name for good reason. Those who read it are to have understanding. The Church today understands Revelation to be an explanation of the Tribulation period. Many teachers say that it's the time of God's wrath. But as we saw in chapter 4, this understanding is confused! We can see in Revelation 6:16 just when God's wrath will be announced as imminent. It's certainly not at the beginning of the Tribulation. As we can see, it is instead at the end of the seals, which many conclude as being the end of the Tribulation. I believe this is correct.

First of all, it is reasonable to believe from the teaching of Scripture that all that went before this verse describing the sixth seal was part of the Tribulation. Yet, wrath is not announced until seal six. The six seals of Revelation chapter 6 seems to parallel our Lord's description of what was to befall us in Matthew 24:5-9. These seals are the beginning of sorrows, and include the death and martyrdom that takes place during the Tribulation. The fifth seal of Revelation 6:9-11, when compared to Matthew 24:9, reveals the result of this death and martyrdom of the Tribulation saints. "Then they will deliver you up to tribulation, and put you to death; and you will be hated by all nations for my name's sake." In the fifth seal, these Tribulation saints who laid down their lives are seen under the altar. Yet Israel has not yet been saved and her judgment—the time of Jacob's trouble, which will bring about her salvation—has not yet begun.

The sixth seal parallels Matthew 24:29, which takes place immediately after the Tribulation. If we look at the wording of that verse, the activities that are taking place correspond to the sixth seal. In both verses we see the heavens being shaken and the darkness encompassing the earth. Mark 13:24 sheds even more light on this as being a period of time prior to the Lord's coming. "But in those days, after that tribulation, the sun will be darkened . . ." We can see here that there will be a period of days *after* the Tribulation, *before* the Lord will return; during those days disastrous events will be occurring.

Revelation is giving us a point-by-point detailed account of what the Lord encapsulated in Matthew 24. Chapter 7 of Revelation confirms that the Tribulation is in its last stages, and that God's wrath is about to be poured out. Here we see the sealing of the 144,000 from the twelve tribes of Israel (Rev. 7:3-4). And we see the saints who have come out of the Tribulation;

therefore the Tribulation is either coming to a close or it's already complete. Yet this is prior to the seven trumpets in sequence of events, and is still prior to Israel's salvation—otherwise the 144,000 would not need to be sealed. Their sealing is for their protection: "'Do not harm the earth or the sea or the trees, till we have sealed the servants of our God upon their foreheads.' And I heard the number of the sealed, a hundred and forty-four thousand . . . "(Rev.7:3). These are all Jews.

The day of the Lord's wrath is at the beginning of the Millennium. This is the day when the earth will move out of her place (Isa.13:9–13), and the day when His feet shall stand upon the Mount of Olives (Zech.14:1–9). These events do not occur, nor could they occur during the Tribulation period. Even great men in recent history have recognized these truths. Dallas Theological Seminary's first president, Louis S. Chafer, wrote concerning the day of the Lord's wrath as follows:

> This lengthened period of a thousand years begins, generally speaking, with the second advent of Christ and the judgments connected therewith, and ends with the passing of the present heaven and the present earth.[2]

Jacob's trouble explained

If the seals mark the end of the Tribulation, as it would seem, how do the trumpets fit in? We either have to conclude, as many do, that the trumpets go back and further explain the Tribulation, or else we have to see them fitting into the days following the Tribulation, which would correspond to Mark's account in chapter 13. The time of Jacob's trouble in Revelation appears to coincide with the seven trumpets which begin with a day of darkness. According to Joel 2:31, "The sun shall be turned into darkness and the moon to blood," but he also says that this will occur "before the great and terrible day of the Lord comes." This coincides with the trumpet judgments, and leads to the destruction of one-third of the earth's population. It will end with the seventh trumpet bringing about the first resurrection (which is the Rapture), and the judgment of the first resurrection dead. Israel's salvation will occur just prior to the first resurrection, concluding the time of Jacob's trouble and Daniel's 70th week.[3]

We need to be sure that we understand just why the trumpet judgments would equate to the time of Jacob's trouble. It's important to see that the trumpet judgments seem to line up with and relate to a period of time immediately following the Tribulation, and immediately preceding the Lord's coming. Now, according to Joel 2, Israel will be in their time of great distress just before the Lord's coming in the day of wrath. The trumpets therefore fit perfectly in Revelation's sequence. The trumpets also bring about an acceleration of destruction upon the earth—thus reminding us that these days must be shortened. But why is earth's destruction accelerating? And why is it happening during Israel's time of trouble? Prophecy requires that great destruction takes place on earth just before the Lord returns. There is a time of wrath that is taught for Israel. The Lord pointed out to the disciples this time of Israel's wrath to the disciples, and we see it recorded in Luke 21:23-24:

> Alas for those who are with child and for those who give suck in those days! For great distress shall be upon the earth and wrath upon this people; they will fall by the edge of the sword, and be led captive among all nations; and Jerusalem will be trodden down by the Gentiles, until the times of the Gentiles are fulfilled.

It's in the very next verses in Luke that we see the heavens shaken and the distress of nations. Men are fainting with fear of what is coming upon the world. The world knows the meaning of Armageddon, and it is the trumpets which call nations to Armageddon.

But Luke's prophecy has a double meaning, as do many other prophecies recorded in Scripture. I believe that the Scripture in Luke would have this prophetic double meaning—for this statement is made by the Lord concerning wrath against Israel at the end of the age; yet, it also had significance for the destruction of Jerusalem in A.D. 70 and for the dispersion in A.D. 135.

But the significance of this prophecy for the end time is that wrath will again be poured out on the house of Jacob. At the time of this outpouring, Israel will still be unsaved, so this is called the time of Jacob's trouble. Calling it this is significant since the patriarch Jacob was not renamed Israel until after his inclusion into the Old Covenant. This implies that once the time of wrath is complete against Israel, she will then be included into the New Covenant; then she can truly claim to be Israel.

Now, we also need to understand that there are divisions of time recorded in Scripture concerning what is occurring surrounding the time of Jacob's trouble. There are 1290 days recorded in Daniel 12:7-12, which creates a link to Revelation 12:12-17. Both of these passages relate to the Tribulation. In Revelation we see Satan cast down to the earth by Michael the Archangel immediately before the 1260 days begin; and in Daniel we see that this same Michael stands aside as the Antichrist is camped outside Jerusalem, which would be at the end of these 1260 days. In other words Michael will cast Satan to the earth and will continue to protect Israel for 1260 days. Then he will move aside just before the battle of Armageddon. In

Revelation, Satan is cast to the earth, and Satan immediately pursues Israel, who is taken into protection for the duration of the Tribulation (1260 days, or three and one half years). "But the woman (Israel) was given the two wings of the great eagle that she might fly from the serpent into the wilderness, to the place where she is to be nourished for a time, and times, and half a time" (Rev.12-14).

Once the Tribulation is complete—now comes the time for Michael to stand aside, as recorded in Daniel 12.[4]

"At that time shall arise (stand aside) Michael, the great prince who has charge of your people. And there shall be a time of trouble, such as never has been since there was a nation till that time; but at that time your people shall be delivered, every one whose name shall be found written in the book" (Dan. 12:1).

This standing aside allows wrath to encompass Israel and begins Jacob's trouble immediately following the Tribulation. Thus Jacob's trouble will then cover approximately 75 days between the Tribulation and the end of Daniel's 70th week. "Blessed is he who waits and comes to the thousand three hundred and thirty-five days" (Dan.12:12).

Why would we have come to this conclusion? Let's back up for a moment. The Lord says to Daniel "at that time" Michael shall stand aside. The term "stand aside" was brought to my attention by Marvin Rosenthal, who, when writing on this same subject from a different point of view, made the following observations: "Rashi, one of Israel's greatest scholars and one who had no concern regarding the issue of the timing of the Rapture . . . understood *stand up* to literally mean *stand still*. The meaning, according to one of Israel's greatest scholars, would be to *stand aside* or *be inactive*. Michael, the guardian of Israel, had earlier fought for her (Dan. 10:13, 21), but now the one 'who standeth for the children of thy [Daniel's] people' would stand still or stand aside. He would not help; he would not restrain; he would not hold down. The Midrash, commenting on this verse, says, 'The Holy One, Blessed be He, said to Michael, you are silent? You do not defend my children'"(Ruth Rabbah I).[5]

Michael will stand aside at a particular time. If we look to Daniel 11:40, we see that this occurs at "the time of the end." The Antichrist has now invaded Israel and is camped outside "the glorious holy mountain," and also at this time his end is near (v. 45). This implies that the armies from the North and East are now gathering against him. This gathering of armies is at Armageddon, and is the end of the Antichrist.

Let's back up for a moment. During this same 1260 days (or three and one-half years) in Revelation, Israel is protected, and we see Satan pursuing the offspring of Israel (the Church). "Then the dragon was angry with the woman, and went off to make war on the rest of her offspring, on those who keep the commandments of God and bear testimony to Jesus" (Rev.12:17). Israel's protection at this time, then, in no way indicates that the Tribulation is the time of Jacob's trouble. It is instead, as we stated in an earlier section, the time for the "shattering of the power of the holy people" (Dan.12:7). And if you will recall, we saw from Scripture that we are the holy people of God in this age; Israel will not bear this title with us until she is saved.

What we see then, following the 1260 days, is an initial, but partial, outpouring of wrath occurring immediately after the tribulation of those days (Matt. 24:29). This is intended to punish Israel and lead her sealed remnant to repentance, and it occurs during the trumpet judgments.

Therefore I will judge you, O house of Israel, every one according to his ways, says the Lord God. Repent and turn from all your transgressions, lest iniquity be your ruin. Cast away from you all the transgressions which you have committed against me, and get yourselves a new heart and a new spirit! Why will you die, O house of Israel? For I have no pleasure in the death of any one, says the Lord God; so turn, and live. (Ezek. 18:30-32)

Looking again to Daniel 12:1, we can see that this time of trouble is for Daniel's people, the nation Israel. Yet from Revelation we can also see that it's a preparation for the wrath of God on the world. It's during this time that the bowls of wrath are poured out. The pouring out of these bowls seems to parallel the days of the first six trumpets. The sixth bowl announces Armageddon and the coming of the Day of the Lord in judgment, whereas the seventh trumpet announces the millennial reign of the Lord (the same event).

Remember this is the same Lord, but He returns with two separate purposes. He returns both to judge and to reign. The winepress is full upon His return as the seventh angel announces "It is done." "Through the wrath of the LORD of hosts the land is burned, and the people are like fuel for the fire . . ." (Isa. 9:19). Two-thirds of Israel will be destroyed during the outpouring of wrath (before the salvation of the nation takes place).

And I will give portents in the heavens and on the earth, blood and fire and columns of smoke. The sun shall be turned to darkness, and the moon to blood, before the great and terrible day of the LORD comes. And it shall come to pass that all who call upon the name of the LORD shall be delivered; for in Mount Zion and in Jerusalem there shall be those who escape, as the LORD has said, and among the survivors shall be those whom the LORD calls (Joel 2:30–32). "For in a very little while my indignation will come to an end, and my anger will be directed to their destruction." (Isa. 10:25)

The "their" in this verse represents the Babylonians, the Assyrians, and other nations who have surrounded Israel.

The destruction of Babylon is foretold many places in Scripture, and her destruction gives us a clue as to when the bowls will have their actual affect on the nations of the earth. Will it be before or after the tribulation? Isaiah chapter 13 predicts the actual fall of Babylon. Verse 9 says that it will occur on the day of the Lord, and it further says that it will be during that day when the Lord will destroy the earth. We might remember that it is that day that is the 1000-year day of the millennium.[6]

But, how does the destruction of Babylon help us predict the effect of the bowls on the earth? First of all, Isaiah 13:10 tells us that this destruction will come after the stars have fallen and the sun is darkened. According to what we have seen from Jesus' teachings in Matthew 24, Mark 13, and Revelation 6:13, this will be after the Tribulation. Yet at the time of the pouring out of the bowls, the Scripture records, "And God remembered great Babylon, to make her drain the cup of the fury of his wrath . . ." (Rev. 16:19). Now, this statement is made immediately after the Lord had said: " Lo, I am coming like a thief! Blessed is he who is awake keeping his garments that he may not go naked and be seen exposed! And they assembled them at the place which is called in Hebrew Armageddon." Babylon's destruction will then come by way of the bowls of God's wrath, and will occur in time sequence *after* the Lord's return to tread the winepress of wrath.

God will use the Antichrist, no matter who he is,

and the battle of Armageddon to judge Israel; but when the act of repentance does occur on Israel's part, it leads to the completion of the olive tree (Rom. 11:24), and the Rapture of all saints who remain. And accompanying the Rapture is, of course, the first resurrection of the dead (1 Cor. 15:51–52; Rom. 11:15).

"In that day the remnant of Israel and the survivors of the house of Jacob will no more lean upon him that smote them, but will lean upon the LORD, the Holy One of Israel, in truth" (Isa. 10:20). Immediately after the rapture of Israel's saints (including the Church), the remaining Jews, those who have not been raptured or killed by the Antichrist and the armies converging against Jerusalem, will either be destroyed among the totally wicked, as the Lord's wrath is poured out, or they will be carried back to Jerusalem on the shoulders of the Gentiles.

These Jews who are carried back are not part of the nation Israel. They therefore are not saved in a day, as will be the survivors of the nation Israel. They however will stand at the bema judgement seat of Christ with all of Israel, including the Church. In Ezekiel we see this occur after the return of the Lord (Ezek.20:33-38). It should be noted that those Jews who are returned unsaved will not be able to enter Israel (v. 38). Remember, Paul says that they are not all Israel who are descended from Israel (Rom. 9:6). We must also see here that at least some of these unsaved Jews are still alive after the Lord returns, after wrath is poured out (v. 33). We must also keep in mind here that in the kingdom, we (the Church) are part of the commonwealth of Israel, and we inherit the covenants.[7] This will be the time of our reward, which is separate from the judgment of the nations (Gentiles). We will look more at the bema judgement later.

This judgment, however, begins to explain who

will be left for the saints to reign over. We had spoken earlier about the Feast of Trumpets in chapter 3. It is Jewish tradition concerning this feast, coupled with Scripture, that supports that tradition which will tell us just who will be left. The Feast of Trumpets was a festival given to the Jews. To the Jew it is called Rosh Hashanah, which is the Jewish New Year. According to Theodore Gaster and other Jewish scholars,[8] the day of Rosh Hashanah involves the sounding of the last trumpet. But more than that, the day itself is seen within the Jewish faith as representing "the 1000-year Millennial reign of Messiah." It is known as "the day of coronation".[9] It also teaches about the "wedding of the Messiah, the rewards of the court, . . . the Day of judgment." This feast also speaks of the day of Jacob's trouble and the resurrection of the dead.[10] All of these things we have seen in Scripture as a part of the seven trumpets of Revelation, which is the day of Jacob's trouble, and which announces the Millennium. The Millennium begins with the resurrection of the dead, the rewarding of the saints, the judgment of the wicked and of the nations, and ends with the second resurrection and the Great White Throne Judgment. And it includes the marriage of the Lamb. All of this is taught by the Jews as part of Rosh Hashanah.

Joseph Good, in his book, *Rosh Hashanah and the Messianic Kingdom to Come*, makes many interesting points concerning this feast. In it he says, "On the day of Rosh Hashanah, each man is judged. G——d has three books that are opened. Those who have returned to G——d are written in the Book of the Righteous . . . All other people are divided into two other groups. The first of these is known as the Rashim, the wholly wicked, and their names are written into a book of the same name. Their fate is sealed on Rosh Hashanah, for they have forever rejected, of their own accord, the salvation of G——d provided through His Messiah.

"The last group is known as the intermediates. These are the common people, and they comprise the largest group. They have not yet been judged righteous, nor have they been placed into the book of the wholly wicked."[11] Good goes on to say that these are given until Yom Kippur to repent.[12] "All things are judged on Rosh Hashanah, and their fate is sealed on Yom Kippur" (Tosefta Rosh Hashanah 1.13). It is this intermediate group, who will be ruled over during the Millennium. We'll see additional scriptural support for this in just a few pages.

Also, it should be noted that since the days are cut short, no one knows just when the seals will end and the trumpets begin; nor can we decipher by pure numbers of days just how much each will overlap the other. All of this only reinforces the fact that the Lord will manipulate this time for the sake of the elect. God is sovereign. Allegorizing, as we have done here, should never be done unless the Lord gives a reason to allegorize; and concerning the days recorded in Revelation and Daniel, as they relate to the Tribulation and time of Jacob's trouble, the reason is clear. His Word calls for it. These days will be shortened.

Just before these days known as Jacob's trouble begin, God will seal 144,000 from the twelve tribes of Israel. They are not sealed to be witnesses as is often taught—nothing is stated about their being witnesses. They are sealed to protect them from the outpouring of the wrath of God on the house of Israel. Remember, they are not yet saved. The day of their salvation, however, has almost come. It will be complete at the end of Daniel's 70th week, which includes, but does not coincide exactly with, the Tribulation period. Remember, the Tribulation is over when the sixth seal is opened. We must also keep in mind that, according to Mark 13, there are days of destruction remaining before the Lord returns to tread the winepress of

God's wrath. This is the literal teaching of Matthew 24:29 and Mark 13:24, and is depicted in Rev. 6:12-13. What we have seen is not only literal, but it doesn't contradict what the Lord taught us in Matthew and Mark concerning the close of the age.

Joel teaches that the desecration of the land of Israel is a warning of the nearness of the Day of the Lord (Joel 1:15-16). This does not mean that the message spoken of during the Tribulation is not a message of terror to Israel.

Immediately following Israel's salvation and the Rapture, the Lord will execute wrath against the nations. Revelation 14:9-11 gives us the truth concerning the wrath of God poured out here against those who will receive the mark of the beast. These will be the "wholly wicked." Notice God's wrath will be poured out in the presence of the Lamb, and this torment will last forever and ever. Again we have confirmation that the Tribulation could not equal this wrath.

Judgement of the nations and the millennial reign

We then come to the place that is referred to in Scripture as the judgment of the nations (we had mentioned this earlier). Just where these nations will come from is again revealed from a literal interpretation of Scripture. They will include the individuals from the nations who favored the saints through the Tribulation, although at first glance it appears that all people and nations will be destroyed at the coming of the King (Rev. 19:17-21). Look just beyond this event to Revelation 20:3, where there is evidence that some are left from the nations. These who are judged worthy will be given an invitation to enter the kingdom or Millennium. This will be the pattern according to the following Scriptures: Matthew 25:31-34, Zech. 14:16-21, Daniel 7:11-14a, Isaiah 45:14-25, and Ezekiel 40-46.

It is evident here that these nations will be ruled with a "rod of iron." The nations who are outside the city during the Millennium (Rev. 22:15) could be the nations who are spoken of here. They are referred to as the dogs (Gentiles), sorcerers, fornicators, and murderers. Why would they be referred to as such? It appears that it is because they're still corrupt. They have not yet accepted Christ as Lord and Savior. They are allowed to remain on earth during the Millennium to be ruled by Christ. They are not bad people, as were the totally wicked, but they are full of dead men's bones. Daniel 7 also confirms this. Beginning with verse 11, we see that the beasts of Daniel's vision were allowed to remain after Christ's second coming, even though their dominion will be taken away. But it's interesting to note that their lives are prolonged for only a season. This season would more than likely be until the end of the Millennium.

These nations are also the ones who must offer sacrifice, since their sins are not covered by the blood of Christ. In Ezekiel, the prophet describes the new temple of the kingdom beginning with chapter 40. Then in chapter 44 and continuing into chapter 46, we see the instructions for the sacrifices to be offered. We can be sure that those sacrifices are to be offered for those other than the sons of God. The clue in Ezekiel as to just who these are is found in chapter 39, verse 21. Here, immediately after the return of the Lord, we see Him establishing Himself among the heathen nations. We saw in Zechariah that these must go up year after year to worship, otherwise plagues will befall them. Again in Isaiah 60:11-13, we read: "Your gates shall be open continually; day and night they shall not be shut; that men may bring to you the wealth of the nations, with their kings led in procession. For the nation and kingdom that will not serve you shall perish; those nations shall utterly be laid waste."

So we see here that God's wrath will continue even during the Millennium. Remember the day of wrath encompasses the entire Millennium. These nations which offer sacrifice are also the nations that will bow down to the nation Israel (Isa. 49:23).

Isaiah 45, beginning with verse 14, is possibly the best depiction that we find in Scripture of the salvation of these nations. We will not quote the entire last half of the chapter here, but a reading of it readily depicts the setting as being millennial. Verse 17 speaks to the salvation of Israel as being complete to "all eternity." Verse 20 speaks of the "survivors of the nations." Verse 22 calls for those survivors to "turn to me and be saved, all the ends of the earth!" In verse 23, every knee will bow to the Lord, and every tongue confess Him.

Unfortunately, it appears that many of these will never come to that saving relationship with Christ, although there will be peace because Satan is bound, for they will rebel as soon as he is loosed. It should be pointed out that there may be some who will come to salvation at this time. It seems that acceptance would allow entry into the city through the gate (Rev. 22: 14), if indeed this Scripture is a true representation of the nations who are judged and outside of Jerusalem during the Millennium.

Now, we can see that which is taught by many dispensationalists, that God's dealing with people differently at different times implies that God has more than one people, is just not supported by Scripture. It cannot be true; we can't have it both ways. We cannot be a part of Abraham and at the same time separate from Abraham. God records in Scripture that all of the saved through all generations are called the saints of God. We don't receive sainthood after we die; sainthood is imputed at the time of the new birth.

Why is all of this important? Because God is preparing a people. We'll discuss this more in the last chapter. But before we do, consider again the events of our day, as nations and governments are now in position to fulfill the prophetic role assigned them. First, peace will be offered, and then there will be the final aggression against Israel. Daniel's prophecy describes the time of the Antichrist as a time when the Arab nations would align under one strong leader. That leader is seen in Scripture as the King of the South. The Antichrist himself could come from this group of nations or from the European Common Market, which is now established and set to begin free trade this year. No matter where he comes from, the New Age will play a vital part in his rise.

The events of our day, although still frightening to many, are pregnant with the signs which Christians look for, and because of this, there is encouragement that God, not man, is in control of the universe.

Lord as judge of all saints

Now, going back to the beginning of the Millennium, the Lord will again be on the earth bodily, but this time as our Judge and King. Having considered the judgment of nations, which occurs immediately upon our Lord's return, we need to consider the judgment of the saints spoken of in Revelation 11:15. You'll recall that in this passage we saw the time of the seventh trumpet that calls us home. The passage records that this is also the time for the dead to be judged. The question here, of course, is evident—just who are these dead who are to be judged? Some would say that this is referring to the final Great White Throne Judgement. Others just ignore this judgment of the dead altogether. Walvoord and Zuck in their commentary acknowledge it, but drop it like a hot potato.[13] Thiessen writes eight pages on the judgments, and references approximately 100 Scriptures, but does not mention this judgment of the dead recorded in Revelation 11:18, not even one time.[14]

But the explanation is in the passage itself explaining just who these are, and is confirmed in 1 Corinthians 4:5 and Romans 9:6–13. They are the servants (the prophets and the saints, the children of the promise) who will be judged. This is the first resurrection. Remember, this is immediately after the acceptance by Israel of the New Covenant. Salvation has now come for the Jewish nation Israel, and the Church is complete. This is the time, according to Acts 3:20 and Romans 11:15, for Israel's repentance, which leads to the resurrection ("life from the dead"), and the Rapture.

This judgment of the dead, being the judgment of the first resurrection dead, is the literal interpretation; and if it is toyed with, it opens the door for error. If we say that this is the judgment of the second resurrection dead, this opens the door for the argument that there will be no Millennium, for the judgment spoken of here comes at the end of the Tribulation. If this is interpreted as final judgment, then how can we argue in support of the Millennium? Of course, the pre-tribulational rapturist cannot admit that this is the judgment of the Church, because the judgment of the Church during the Tribulation is seen by him as having already occurred, and is one of the reasons presented by him to show why it is necessary to have the Rapture prior to the Lord's Second Coming.[15]

But why does the pre-tribulational teacher not see this? Consider the fact that he believes that this judgment will take a long time. And he also believes that the Marriage Supper has occurred in chapter 19 before the revelation of Christ. Yet, two things should be considered. First, in Revelation 19 the Marriage Supper is only announced, and this announcement does not mean that it has to or will take place before the end of the Tribulation. It merely states to us that everything is now ready. And this readiness is announced immediately before the Lord's return to this earth. This then is not an unusual announcement. We have already seen that this announcement is actually made at the time of the Rapture. Further proof of this is seen in the parable of the wedding feast.

Second, Peter offers us even more scriptural support for interpreting this literally as the judgment of those of the first resurrection (the saints, including the Church). Listen: "Therefore gird up your minds, be sober, set your hope fully upon the grace that is coming to you at the revelation of Jesus Christ" (1 Pet.1:13). Peter recognizes that at the time of the Lord's return, you and I will need to draw on all of God's grace. Now, I have pointed out to you several times the distinction between the Rapture and the revelation which is made in the minds of the pre-tribers. The revelation is the time of the Lord's actual return to the earth (not according to me, but according to them). Of course, on this point, they are correct; but then this makes this passage of Scripture even more significant, since the Lord says here (almost in defiance of their view) that it is at the time of the revelation of Christ that we will need grace to sustain us for judgment (also see 1 Cor. 4:5). How can we need grace at the revelation of Christ to this earth if we are already raptured and judged prior to His coming to earth?

This judgment, in fact, will not take place until after we are raptured and have returned with Christ. We spoke of this earlier as the bema judgment seat. This judgement is pictured by Ezekiel (Ezek.20:33-38).

Here we are standing before the "King" "face to face" at a time when "wrath" has been "poured out." This has to be after the Second Coming and the treading of the winepress. Therefore we are now a part of the commonwealth of Israel, and heirs to the covenants (Eph.2:11-14). This then is the actual picture of the bema judgment seat of Christ.

All that we've seen from the literal interpretation of Scripture is confirmed as our spirits bear witness with God's spirit. He takes away the confusion which certainly was not of Him but of Satan. I hope that by this time I've not only aroused, but that the Holy Spirit has satisfied much of your curiosity. Remember not even the pre-tribulationalist disagrees with us on the fact that the saints will be judged.

ELEVEN

WAKE UP MY BRETHREN

"Awake, and strengthen what remains and is on the point of death, for I have not found your works perfect in the sight of my God. Remember then what you received and heard; keep that, and repent. If you will not awake, I will come like a thief, and you will not know at what hour I will come upon you" (Rev. 3:2-3).

I believe that the Church, if not blind, must certainly be asleep. We've been asleep to the workings of Satan through the New Age movement; a movement which brought rise to Hitler, and now is proclaiming the coming of the New Age messiah, the Lord Maitreya; a movement which believes that the Church must be done away with in order to allow the new order of evolved man to take over; a movement which has been behind disarmament in order to usher in the so-called era of peace; a movement which teaches that the Church and the Jew, who represent separatist thought, must be "cleansed" (their word for destroyed), before this peace can come. According to them, those who will not accept Maitreya (or the new David) must be cleansed. We can't stop the coming of Antichrist, nor would we want to. He will come in God's timing, but we must be awake and prepare.

Now, I am not condemning you, for neither have I always been awake. The wool has been pulled over our eyes. But, how does that happen? Dave Hunt gives testimony in his book of his early interest in prophecy. Listen:

> I became convinced at a young age that there were a number of coming events which had been prophesied so clearly in Scripture that one could be absolutely certain they would take place. Foremost among these, of course, was the rapture of the church, an event which, as I have already explained, we believed could occur at any moment. I looked forward to it with dread in those early days because I had not yet received the Lord Jesus Christ as my personal Savior.[1]

Dave Hunt may give us a clue here as to just how we've allowed this teaching to influence us. Preachers have presented it as scriptural fact in order to influence our salvation, and we have believed it due to the fact that it came from preachers who have led us to the Lord. I was raised in a Southern Baptist church, where this teaching was prevalent. I too had this same fear, and believed this same doctrine before I had accepted the Lord. Yet, the ministry that the Lord used to save me was Dave Wilkerson's ministry. I was saved in the living room of my home while reading his book *The Cross and the Switchblade*. As I read more of Dave Wilkerson's works, I found that he did not hold to this same doctrinal position on the Rapture. Who was right? I trusted my church, but I also trusted Dave Wilkerson. Perhaps this is the way God chose to work in my life for a reason. Today I'm not certain if Dave Wilkerson is totally correct, but I am certain that Scripture is totally correct.

Putting this book together has been quite an experience, as the Lord has involved me in several situations which all taken together have been quite eye-opening. Many books have been read as the Lord has immersed me in one volume after another. One such book was written by a former insider of the New Age movement, Randall Baer. He had been a naturopathic doctor within the movement, and had become an international authority to the disciples of the New Age. His book, published by Huntington House, entitled *Inside the New Age Nightmare*, gives first hand knowledge of the growing threat to Christianity. Having forsaken all that he knew, including his profession, in order to become a Christian, certainly his views can't be ignored concerning the Second Coming. I found them to be an encouragement to me concerning the direction that the Holy Spirit was leading me in the writing of this book. Mr. Baer stated it this way:

> A portion of the testimony that the Lord has laid upon my heart is to add my small voice to that of so many Christians who have felt the quickening of the Holy Spirit in knowing for certain that the personal and visible return of Jesus draws near. Our blessed hope is close at hand as the Lord of lords and King of kings comes on the clouds of the sky with power and great glory to cast down the abominable Antichrist, gather the faithful and to institute the long-awaited millennium that He has promised.[2]

There certainly isn't much that one could add to what Mr. Baer had said, other than to state that others will certainly be called upon to give their lives for the cause of Christ even as he has done. You see, Randall Baer lost his life upon the release of his book. Satan's wrath is already kindled against works such as Mr. Baer's and the one that you're currently reading.

Another situation which arose during this writing involved my contact with a Jehovah's Witness. I'm quite frankly sorry to say that ordinarily I wouldn't have given as much effort to the winning of a Jehovah's Witness as I did in this case. My personal knowledge of this situation, however, caused me to be concerned for the entire family's salvation. The events that followed in weeks to come were, as I now look back on them, certainly of the Lord.

One of the "witnessing" gifts to me from this family was a 1987 Watchtower publication entitled *Revelation: Its Grand Climax at Hand*. The book certainly was a real revelation as to just how deceived a person and group can be. But even more important, it opened my eyes to the far-reaching impact that Satan's plan is having, and to the many different sources he is using to push his plan to conclusion.

The scenario that Satan has set up with the Jehovah's Witness group, though much different in approach, still produces the same final outcome as would the most avowed New Ager's demonic plan.

First of all, the entire theological scheme presented to the Jehovah's Witness' "great crowd" (those who are not a part of the 144,000 saved John Class"), is constantly changing as new light is being shed upon Scripture. This may sound innocent enough, but think of it. Satan can drive this entire cult in any direction he sees fit as time progresses and the need arises to do so. They claim to be people of the Word; however, their interpretation of it is anything but literal, and therefore they become subject to any deceptive spirit.

The foundation of this organization was laid in opposition to the Church on the principle "come out from among them." The true Church as we know it is seen by Jehovah's Witnesses as a part of "Christendom" as a whole. And you who have studied or even just read on the New Age plan of Satan will recognize, as I describe the teachings of the "John Class", the infiltration of New Age thought into their theology. For here within their theology, we see that the beast of Revelation, who to them is the Antichrist, is none other than Christendom itself. The Jehovah's Witnesses have now come out of her. They also see the Jew and other "false religions" of the world to be a part of the whore riding upon the back of the beast. The main emphasis as you study their teaching on Revelation is anti-Christendom. This theme overshadows any and all other themes. Christendom is renounced for its "false teaching" on the Trinity, predestination, and hell, just to name a few.

The time of tribulation, which Scripture says is yet future, in the mind of a Jehovah's Witness is almost over. According to them, Revelation's prophecies have been fulfilled in our generation. Christ is said to have received His throne in 1914, and is carrying out His wrath against the Church during this day of the Lord. Christendom has since the beginning of that day in 1914 persecuted the Jehovah's Witness as described in elaborate detail throughout this twisted work. But believe me, they haven't seen anything yet in compari-son to what Satan has in store for them. It's obvious that Satan has used the apostate church to color their entire image of the Church "Beastly." This makes it very difficult, but not impossible, to reach them.

What of their opinion of the Jew in God's plan? They have been replaced by the "true Christian." And they of course are the true Christian. The true Chris-tian is Jehovah's chosen people. The Messiah, they say, is not God, but "a god." He is Michael the Archangel, called Jesus the Son of God. All of this is very revealing to the believer.

Where does it all lead the Jehovah's Witness in terms of future events? What will happen to them at the revealing of the Antichrist or false messiah who is soon planned as part of the New Age by Satan? It appears from their own teaching that when the Anti-christ steps forth and sets himself up as God in the temple, the witnesses will more than likely follow him not as the Antichrist but as God.

Why are they so deceived? Because much of what they teach sounds right. It is right out of Scripture. Remember Satan also uses Scripture, but to his advantage. His use of Scripture will deceive if possible the very elect, and certainly those who are not born of the Spirit have no chance against his wiles. This is why the teaching of the Word has to be literal, and all of Scripture has to be tied into our doctrine.

Unfortunately this group is unaware that it is being manipulated toward total involvement in the New Age. Consider what Lola Davis has to say in her book, *Toward a World Religion for the New Age,* where she is pointing out "The good news . . . that there is already much activity toward required actions and conditions and that an increasing number of people are *either consciously or unconsciously* preparing mankind for a World Religion that's compatible with the New Age."[3]

Now I'm certainly not all wise, and certainly not perfect. My understanding is not based on all knowledge, but God is faithful and if He commands that we be awake, then He will keep us awake and out of darkness if we heed His command. We can only desire to know His truth and follow the leading of His Holy Spirit. If I close my mind to His truth, shame on me! I must remember that His truth is not contrary to the teaching of His Word. You must do the same.

I'm praying for those that God has put in my path, those who we certainly can see are deceived. But are they seeking for the truth? I'm praying that somehow each will find Jesus who is the only truth. It's because of this great deception that a blindness has set in, and I can't impact this situation without the help of Almighty God.

Another interesting event happened to me recently as I was visiting the home office of a company with whom I'm associated. The trip was to attend a meeting, the purpose of which was to introduce various functions in His company to the future in records storage and retrieval. The seminar itself was conducted by Kodak. That's right! The same Kodak that presents "Captain EO" at Epcot Center. This presentation was revealing. The video and slide presentation that they put on reconfirmed their dedication to "Spaceship Earth." Kodak's concept of our future is bright. They visualize a world of freedom where information is and should be shared on a worldwide basis. Their systems and products are focused on just this kind of world. The products displayed were what you and I would consider futuristic. However it soon became apparent that the future is NOW. Kodak, in cooperation with companies such as IBM and DEC, had created systems that would allow the computer to draw on data bases anywhere in the world and would bring them together under one roof as they are accessed by a single personal computer. Right now there's only one thing missing in their network, and for that they're voicing strong support. The missing link is what they call "open systems." Open systems will allow data to be accessed by any and all who need and are approved to use them. You and I need not use much imagination to understand what use the New Age can make of this tool once it's in place.

Now, add what I've just described to other new technologies of our day, and no one is truly free. Consider the new government spy satellite recently launched. With it comes a boast that a license plate can be read from outer space. Are you remembering Daniel's prophecy? Remember it says that its message will be sealed until the end and then men will run to and fro, and knowledge will increase. Are we awake?

Needless to say, I wasn't at all surprised to find my host viewing our world as standing on the threshold of a major breakthrough toward peace. The Lord had

allowed me to be in a one-on-one situation with this
Ph.D. and former professor from a major mid-western
university. He is now in charge of information storage
and retrieval for a major corporation. Coincidence?

He further elaborated on the use of the computer itself as the tool which holds great promise for
our future advancement into this new age of promise.
I was reminded of what Lola Davis envisioned as
coming through education as man "will have developed god-like qualities and sufficient knowledge and
wisdom to cooperate with God in materializing the
Kingdom of God . . ."[4] Obviously not the kingdom for
which you and I wait.

Now, if in fact the things that I have been exposed
to since beginning this book are not God's doing, then
just what is the point? If we consider that most Christian writers, those who've written exposing the New
Age, have pointed out that this movement is not one
begun by man. You can't, in fact, point to any one man
or organization as its originator, but instead it's obvious that men from all walks of life are seeing the same
vision of the "New Age." So we have to admit that
either God or Satan must be involved in the orchestra-
tion of this movement. We must be aware of its spread
throughout our society. This satanic "enlightenment"
is certainly why intelligent men are seeing us as being
on the brink of something new; something phenom-
enal; yes, and something even "miraculous," as Ken
Keys, Jr., describes the transformation that will take
place as our society moves into a higher level of
consciousness. Unfortunately, however, the miracle is
one of deceit for the New Ager. Intelligent men
leaning unto their own understanding are being duped.

Yes, the most intelligent men, such as Dr. Frank
R. Wallace, a former Senior Research Chemist for E.I.
du Pont, de Nemours & Co., are seeing exciting things
ahead. Dr. Wallace has discovered a "new knowledge"

known as "Neo-Tech." Contained in his sixteen page News Report are many interesting bits of information. There's one statement, however, that lets one recognize from just where this man has gleaned his discovery. He concludes: "I now know the full meaning of the Neo-Tech discovery and its power: All will yield to the new-breed Neo-Tech person, the no-limit man or woman . . . Truly great days are coming."[5] In addition, I discovered within his literature that this information is not to be sold to "clergymen and other . . . neocheaters."[6]

The amazing but not so surprising fact is that men of higher education and obvious exposure to the Scriptures are so blind to the evidences presented in Scripture. These scriptural statements are filled with the signs of our time—these signs are leading not to a utopian society on earth (not yet), but to the coming of Antichrist. These signs point to an era of Satan's deceit which leads to the giving over of millions and even billions of souls to a reprobate mind. From all indications we're entering that era today, and as it progresses even the very elect will stand in danger of being deceived. Only our prayerful reliance on God's Word literally understood will keep us away from deception.

One very knowledgeable scholar, as well as an authority on the New Age, has recognized the need for the Church to be alert in our day. Dr. Norman Geisler of Liberty University has, because of his concern, become an expert on the false religions confronting Christianity today. Having read some of his messages the question is: has he gone far enough? I say this having heard him speak extensively on this subject. Now, he recognizes the New Age attacks on Christianity, yet there's no identification of this system with prophecy. He treats it as just another device of Satan to challenge the Church. His advice to us is not to get

excited or carried away, after all we're not looking for
the kingdom of Antichrist, but for the Kingdom of
The Christ.[7]

As an expert, one would think that Dr. Geisler
would be aware of the teachings within the New Age
concerning the need for the purging of a large seg-
ment of Christians and Jews, for many of us will refuse
to be initiated into this false religious system. He even
reluctantly recommends Constance Cumbey's book,
Hidden Dangers of the Rainbow. Although he commends her on her extensive research into the New Age
movement, saying that she has perhaps done the most
extensive research on the subject, he gives a warning
concerning her conclusions. And perhaps she has
implicated some folks that she should not have. However, we should not let this detract us from the factual
truths that she has discovered. These truths are quoted
from the New Age leaders themselves concerning the
future purpose surrounding the purging of the earth.
These leaders point out that the earth must be purged
before the New Age can arrive. Yet Dr. Geisler skirts
this issue in his teaching.

Now, my inquisitive mind causes me to ask, why?
Why does one, who is obviously an expert on this
subject, play down the obvious, as well as the most
threatening and revealing bit of information on this
movement? This is information that links the New Age
through the prophesies of Revelation in such a way
that it becomes very difficult to deny its direct prophetic tie to the Babylonian Antichrist system. As a
matter of fact, it's this link to prophecy that makes this
movement possibly one of the most significant prophetic signs of our day—and I might add, one of the
most dangerous forces to ever enter the pages of
history.

But back to the question—why? Certainly we
don't know for sure. Is it blindness? I don't think so,

yet it could be, for many times our theological position, or our traditional belief, causes us to close our mind to truth. Think of it—if Dr. Geisler believes that the Church will not be here, why should this potential threat concern him, or us?

But the real question is this: is his position logical? Here we have Dr. Geisler, who is one of the most astute apologists on scriptural truth, defending the Scriptures from a literal standpoint, yet refusing to see truth concerning the Second Coming, as well as the signs that line up with Scripture, in his warnings. It's thus becoming even clearer to me that the fulfillment of the times of the Gentiles is bringing in a blindness upon even the very elect. But this is exactly what happened to the Jewish religious system just prior to our Lord's first coming, and it seems to be what would happen to the Church, and possibly even more so as we approach the time of the end.

Consider the Lord's message to Sardis:

> If you will not awake, I will come like a thief, and you will not know at what hour I will come upon you. Yet you have still a few names in Sardis, people who have not soiled their garments; and they shall walk with me in white, for they are worthy. He who conquers shall be clad thus in white garments, and I will not blot his name out of the book of life; I will confess his name before my Father and before his angels. (Rev. 3:3b-5)

TWELVE

THE WEIGHT OF EVIDENCE

Imagine you are now seated on a jury, and now will be presented to you the closing arguments. The closing arguments are crucial in a trial. This is where there have been innocent men convicted of crimes that they didn't commit, and guilty men acquitted of crimes which they did. Let's recap the evidence as Scripture presents it:

1. The Scriptures state that we will all be caught up to be with the Lord in the air—at the last trumpet, after the dead in Christ rise (1 Cor. 15:51–54). With this fact most of the sides agree. Our disagreement is on the timing.

2. This last trumpet is recorded as occurring at the beginning of the Lord's millennial reign, which is after the Great Tribulation (Rev. 11:15–17). The pre-trib rapturist disagrees on this point, seeing it at the beginning, as recorded in Revelation 4:1.

3. There is a mystery surrounding the resurrection (I Cor. 15:51), which is revealed with the sounding of the seventh trumpet of Revelation 11:15 (Rev. 10:7). The pre-trib position disagrees on this point and ignores this evidence.

4. The resurrection and Rapture is pictured when the Tribulation is complete (Matt. 24:15-31).

The pre-trib rapturist also disagrees on this point, and gives no literal scriptural basis.

5. The resurrection of the dead, which immediately precedes the Rapture (see fact one) will occur at the acceptance of Christ as Messiah by the nation Israel. This happens in one day at the end of Daniel's 70th week (Dan. 9:24; Rom. 11:15; Dan. 12:1). This evidence is ignored by both pre-trib and mid-trib teaching, and is seen by pre-trib theologians as either a spiritual resurrection, or one part of the many-part first resurrection. Thus it is not believed literally, nor is it taught correctly; this resurrection is for the Church, and all who are a part of her at the time of Israel's salvation.

6. The Tribulation occurs prior to the end of Daniel's 70th week (Matt.24:29; Rev. 6:12-17; Mark 13:24-25; Joel 2:11 & 3:14-16).

7. Israel will call the Lord her husband in that day (the Millennium), making her a part of the Bride (Hos. 2:16). This is seen as a term of endearment by the pre-trib teachers, and is otherwise ignored by them and others.

8. The Church is called the Bride of Christ (2 Cor. 11:2). On this point all agree.

9. In that day (the Millennium), the Lord will be one and His name one, therefore He cannot have two wives (Zech. 14:9). On this point there is no disagreement.

10. Israel is promised God's wrath (Joel), but the Church is not intended for wrath. Israel will experience this wrath as one third of mankind dies, while the Church (the saints) will experience man's wrath and the wrath of Satan (Rev. 12:12; 13:10; & 14:12). The pre-trib position makes the Tribulation equal to the day of God's wrath. The mid-trib position makes the last half of the Tribulation equal to the day of wrath. Again a literal interpretation is avoided.

11. The day of God's wrath will punish all wicked and therefore cannot be equivalent to the Tribulation period (Rev. 14:9–11; Rom. 2:8–9; Eph. 5:5–6; 1 Thess. 5:9). The opposing positions ignore this fact.

12. God is creating one new man from the Jewish and Gentile believers (Eph. 2:11-19; Jn.11:47-52). The pre-trib position recognizes this fact as reality today, but does away with it during the Tribulation. The Reformed theologians and the reconstructionists both believe this, but ignore the nation Israel's spiritual rebirth and a literal millennium.

13. The fact that Israel and the Church are one is further supported by the titles accorded them. Israel in the Old Testament and the Church in the New are called the *ekklesia* and the saints. In fact, the Hebrew equivalent of *ekklesia* is used more times in the Old Testament to describe Israel than in the New describing the Church. Further evidence is seen in the New Testament as both are termed the elect of God. Not only are the saints seen in the Old Testament (Dan. 7:27; Prov. 2:8; several places in the Psalms) and several places in the New Testament, but several places within the Tribulation. The saints in each of these instances are defined differently by the different positions, yet are one in God's plan.

14. According to Matthew 24, prior to the end of the age, the gospel must be preached to the entire world. We see this occur in Revelation (Rev.14:6), in the midst of what most call the Tribulation, we see the gospel proclaimed "to every nation tribe and tongue." This could not have been fulfilled prior to this time, nor could it have been fulfilled without the presence of the Church (Matt.28:20)!

15. According to Exodus 23:16, God requires two celebrations for harvest. First Fruits sees its fulfillment in the resurrection of Messiah, according to most scholars. But Ingathering is celebrated with the Feast

of Booths, which takes place in the seventh month. It is a one-time event, which according to I Corinthians 15:23 is fulfilled in "those who are Christ's at His coming." Since this is fulfillment of a Jewish feast, it only stands to reason that the Jews will be included as fulfillment of this harvest. This point is ignored by the two-part rapture theories.

16. All three (Israel, the Church, and Tribulation saints) are promised to rule with Christ (Dan. 7:15–28; Rev. 20:4; 1 Cor 6: 1–3). Israel and the Church will be the Bride of Christ at this time (Hos. 2:14–19: 2 Cor. 11:2).

17. Christ will rule with a rod of iron over the heathen nations for 1000 years (Dan. 7:11–14; Rev. 20; Zech. 14:16–21). Christ is to rule over the saved of the Tribulation period by the pre-trib teachers. Yet the Scriptures teach that these will rule with Christ (see point 14—Rev. 20:4). Others spiritualize this literal teaching.

18. Satan and his followers will be cast into the lake of fire which burns forever and ever at the end of the 1000 years (Rev. 20). Most agree on this point, although Reformed and reconstructionist positions do not believe in the literal 1000 years.

A summary of all scriptural evidence says that the Church must be completed through the preaching of the gospel and the salvation of Israel. It definitely teaches that the Rapture will occur after the resurrection of the dead, and that the dead will not be raised until Israel is saved or made part of the Church (the Bride). This is accomplished through the New Covenant. Thiessen makes a statement which is surprisingly supportive of this scriptural summary, but which is totally contradictory to his own position. In this quote taken from the section of the book entitled *Lectures in Systematic Theology*, he states: "It may be added that he (God) has only one plan and that all must be saved in the same way, if they are to be saved at all, whether they be moral or immoral, trained or untrained, Jew or Gentile, whether living in the Old Testament period or in the present age."[1] The truth of this statement by Thiessen is fully supported by Scripture, as we have seen. Why then do men of his persuasion forsake this truth, in fact denying it in their teaching of the separation of the Church and Israel at the time of the Rapture?

If you will recall at the beginning of chapter one, I had put forth for your consideration a premise. It stated that Israel and the Church are one. I believe that what I've recorded in this book based on the Word of God supports this fact. If these Scriptures are true, God has only one covenant people who will inherit the kingdom and receive the benefits of all three covenants. I believe the truth of Scripture and I believe that Scripture proves, therefore, that the Church is a continuation of God's chosen people, a people who were, just as we are, the called-out-ones of God.

Many others in our own times have recognized the dangers of our present day. Heresy and deceit were the dangers seen by the writers of *The Agony of Deceit*, to which Michael Horton contributed and edited.

> Motives are relative. The apostle Paul speaks of people who preach the truth, but with wrong motives. That is better than people who preach heresy with sound motives. We do not doubt for one moment that some of those we are including in our criticism are sincere, compassionate, and genuinely concerned to build up their followers. But judging their motives is beyond our competence. Judging glaring distortions of biblical teaching is not. . . . Such an unhappy task can only be taken up when the issues are clear and the stakes are high.[2]

Another saint, who not only saw the high stakes but the danger of the teaching of a premature Rapture, was Corrie Ten Boom who is now with the Lord:

> There are some among us teaching there will be no tribulation, that the Christians will be able to escape all of this. These are the false teachers Jesus was warning us to expect in the latter days. Most of them have little knowledge of what is already going on across the world.

> I have been in countries where the saints are already suffering terrible persecution. In China the Christians were told, "don't worry, before the tribulation comes, you will be translated—raptured." Then came a terrible persecution. Millions of Christians were tortured to death. Later I heard a bishop from China say, sadly, "We have failed. We should have made the people strong for persecution rather than telling them Jesus would come first." Turning to me he said "You still have time. Tell the people how to be strong in persecution, how to stand when the tribulation comes-to stand and not faint."[3]

These are strong words from a very well-respected saint, one who had seen great hardship in her own life, having suffered in a German concentration camp for her convictions.

We must repent of the teaching of erroneous doctrine before it's too late. It's not that we're not forewarned concerning the error that would creep in. But the question is, should we continue to heed it? Dave MacPherson concluded his book with the following: "In light of the evidence I have prayerfully and carefully given in this book relative to the Pre-Trib origin (which origin has been hidden for a long time), I hereby ask all Bible teachers to declare a moratorium on such teaching—at least until they can check this out for themselves."[4]

Even prior to reading Dave's book, which was given me in August of 1990 by Mickey Brafford, a dear Christian brother, I had been involved in doing just as MacPherson suggested. And having seen all of the evidence, my conclusion must be stronger than his. This doctrine of the Rapture prior to the end of the Tribulation is not a Scriptural teaching, and men and pastors, who will be judged by the very words which they speak, should cease its teaching as a biblical doctrine. Remember James says that "we all make many mistakes." Let's at least undo the ones that are obvious.

THIRTEEN

WHAT TO LOOK FOR &
HOW TO PREPARE!

I want you to know, brethren, that our fathers were all under the cloud, and all passed through the sea, and all were baptized into Moses in the cloud and in the sea, and all ate the same supernatural food and all drank the same supernatural drink. For they drank from the supernatural Rock which followed them, and the Rock was Christ. Nevertheless with most of them God was not pleased; for they were overthrown in the wilderness.

Now these things are warnings for us, not to desire evil as they did. Do not be idolaters as some of them were; as it is written, "The people sat down to eat and drink and rose up to dance."We must not indulge in immorality as some of them did, and twenty-three thousand fell in a single day. We must not put the Lord to the test, as some of them did and were destroyed by serpents; nor grumble, as some of them did and were destroyed by the Destroyer. Now these things happened to them as a warning, but they were written down for our instruction, upon whom the end of the ages has come. Therefore let any one who thinks that he stands take heed lest he fall. (1 Cor.10:1-12)

Therefore, brethren, be the more zealous to confirm your call and election, for if you do this you will never fall; so there will be richly provided for you an entrance into the eternal kingdom of our Lord and Savior Jesus Christ. (2 Pet. 1:10-11)

And they have conquered him by the blood of the Lamb and by the word of their testimony, for they loved not their lives even unto death. (Rev. 12:11)

The Lord Jesus warned us to watch out for false prophets (Matt.7:15). In these last days, heresy abounds within the Church-doctrines of demons, who are masters of deceit.

Even though we know that the time is growing very near for the purging to come, we have not set dates for these things, nor is it my purpose to attempt to do so. We will, however, say this—Christians who are children of light should know the signs, and they should not be ignorant of the times and of the seasons. God has always shown the way to His people. We can see from Scripture that the early Church saw that the greatest sign of the Lord's coming would be the revealing of the Antichrist. The Lord, as well as Daniel and the apostle Paul, emphasized this as being the most important sign, and one to be highly considered when reading the signs.

So, what should we look for? First, the Scriptures teach a massive regathering of Jews to Israel. "For behold, days are coming, says the Lord, when I will restore the fortunes of my people, Israel and Judah, says the Lord, and I will bring them back to the land which I gave to their fathers, and they shall take possession of it" (Jer.30:3). "Set up waymarks for yourself, make yourself guideposts; consider well the highway, the road by which you went. Return O virgin Israel, return to these your cities" (Jer.31:21).

If we are alert we can see this regathering is under way even now, and in fact has been underway for the last half- century. We should also look for this world leader to rise out of the system and philosophies of ancient Rome. He will come forth with a peace plan, and then will actually set himself up as God. He may already be present on earth. Certainly the system in which Satan plans to bring him has been with us since early history, and is spreading its power like never before. However, we are not to take world leaders and turn them into the Antichrist. The Antichrist will be *revealed* in due time, not *discovered* before.

Hal Lindsay, who we have quoted before within the pages of this book, also sees the coming of the Antichrist as being an important sign to watch for at this time: "The only major prophetic sign that is not yet visible is the appearance of the Antichrist and the False Prophet."[1]

Preceding the coming of Antichrist, there will be an increased interest in peace for this world—peace from turmoil and war. Economic chaos could very well permeate the entire world prior to this coming evil one. Cries will go out for disarmament. The great cry will be for unification of world leadership, possibly under the United Nations. I believe that we are already seeing the prelude to these events. The Communist world has all but collapsed due to economic chaos. The Western world has and will continue to borrow greatly against a shaky future. If this is that time, the future will grow more and more bleak for this earth and for her population. Famine and pestilence will increase.

These things, all of which are spoken of in Scripture, will set the stage for the Antichrist and his system of government. Men are already reading the signs and calling for corrective action on the part of the human race. But they ignore God, who is our only salvation from total destruction. And instead of seeing God as the answer to creation's problem, mankind sees Him as the creation in need of man's help. Somehow Satan has twisted conventional thinking to the point that man is God and therefore the savior of this earth.

Additionally, we should look for an awakening of Israel, and their renewed interest in the coming of Messiah. This is already happening, and will culminate in faith during great distress surrounding Israel. If we look to Hosea 14 and Malachi 3&4, the call of the Lord is for Israel's repentance so that He may return to her and heal her. Israel's awakening therefore will be a sign of the coming resurrection. I believe that the Church will play a major role in this awakening, as Israel observes the dedication of the Church to Israel's Messiah and the commitment of the saints to Israel's protection.

It is during these days that many are looking for the Temple to be rebuilt, which would lead to the reestablishment of sacrifices (these will be cut off at the middle of the Tribulation by the Antichrist). It's true that this will probably occur, explaining the prophecies concerning the Antichrist and his act of abomination.

World events are drastically changing. What is God doing in our day to bring about what we have seen from Scripture? In the things to transpire with regard to world events, I see two possible scenarios for the United States. First, The United States and her allies could have less and less influence on the world militarily as a result of the 1991 Persian Gulf war, and the potential for future economic chaos. Why would I say this at a time when it appears that the United States is the world's policeman (the sole remaining super-power)? Consider this: if this war has caused a depletion of our stockpiles of weapons, and if our Congress chooses to not rebuild our armaments, then as the 10-

member system, which will bring in the Antichrist, views this degeneration, it will find it necessary to increase or centralize its own military might. In the future, watch those nations from ancient Rome who seem to be increasing militarily—for the beast must increase in power.

In the second scenario, we see the United States with her roots deeply imbedded in Rome. While all of the world is praising the U.S. as the mighty warrior, this warrior could be entering into a major role in prophecy. This country, whether or not it remains strong economically, could still fulfill the role of the beast-carrying mystery Babylon the Great (Rev.17:5). This beast will support the actual Babylonian religious system made up of the false religious systems of the world, which encompass the entire world's religious philosophy. The seven heads seem to offer a double meaning (possibly representing the continents of the earth), as well as seven kings. "This calls for a mind with wisdom: the seven heads are seven mountains on which the woman is seated, they are also seven kings . . ." (Rev.17:9-10a.).

The *World Book Encyclopedia* lists seven continents and eleven major world religions. If we subtract Christianity from these eleven, we have 10 false religions. Could this harlot be the New Age, which attempts to incorporate all of these world religions into one?

Yet, the harlot described as Babylon the Great is described in Revelation 18 sounding much like a rich economic system, where trade is carried on and wealth is abused. Her destruction will be mourned by the merchants of the sea, who have grown rich because of her. If the United States is able to accomplish peace in Israel in the near future, she will certainly be the best candidate to meet Revelation's description of the beast carrying this harlot.

"And the beast which was and is not, is himself also an eighth, and is one of the seven, and he goes to destruction" (Rev.17:11). The beast associated with Mystery Babylon in Revelation "was and is not." If we examine the "was," we would have to return to the ancient world. The tower of Babel is a significant event in the history of this Beast system. At the tower of Babel the language was one, and apparently the world was in one accord. God said that if this situation were allowed to continue that the people would accomplish whatever their minds imagined. Today the conditions are again right for men to be of one accord and to communicate as one. It is significant that in this day, once again the mystery religion is spreading. Has God allowed all of these conditions to come together in our day for a purpose? Only time will tell.

If we consider that the United States is a melting pot of all ten false religious systems, which could represent the New Age movement, and that these come to us from across the globe and include all seven continents, then we can see a potential correlation between Mystery Babylon, the Beast, and this country. If we further consider that the U.S. is right now attempting to unite North America as one economic entity, then we could certainly represent one of the seven.

We should be aware that the revival of Rome is possibly represented in the spread of democracy eastward. The spread of eastern religion westward is most assuredly the revival of Mystery Babylon's religious arm. The politic of our nation is deeply rooted in Rome. Henry Steele Commager argues and largely proves the influence of the ancient world and more especially Rome on the minds of the men who established our form of government.[2] These men were convinced that this society would go beyond the destructive mistakes of ancient society with a system that would have universal impact on our world for ages to come![s] Could it be that the impact of our government will be world-wide, leading to the coming Antichrist?

We must remember that the United States is not the salvation of the world, nor can she be the pride of the Christian. Our founders are represented by Christian leaders as having been committed men of faith. Yet, among these were men such as John Adams, Ben Franklin, and Thomas Jefferson who did not accept God's Messiah. If you go to Monticello (the home of Jefferson) you will see Jefferson's version of the Scriptures. This has become known as the *Jefferson Bible*. It was rewritten because Jefferson could not accept the Bible as wholly inspired by God. His concept of God was pantheistic. That's right—the New Age god was his god, yet, many of our pastors beat their pulpits claiming these men to have founded a Christian nation, and Jefferson is the writer of the Declaration of Independence.

I appreciate and thank God for the freedom offered in America to worship as we see fit, but in her also is the freedom to learn of Buddha and Krishna and, yes, even of Maitreya, the New Age Antichrist. The roots of America's religious heritage stretch back to Mystery Babylon. Oh, there were Christians among the first settlers, but remember a little leaven leaventh the whole lump, and in our case we see much leaven. But, the real issue is this, is this leaven spreading? David Wilkerson, in *Set the Trumpet to Thy Mouth*, says, "Let the pillow prophets smile condescendingly at our holy rage and our urgent cries of judgment. Not one of them can hinder God's plan to chastise this godless nation."[4] When we consider that this same Jefferson, who rewrote the Bible, drafted the Declaration of Independence, then you can see that our foundation is anything but Christian. Although God has used our freedom for the Church to reach out with the message of Jesus to an uninformed world, God also used ancient Babylon, but that did not spare her from judgment. While some scenario is presently being set up, Russia remains a military powerhouse, even though she is economically bankrupt. Her economic plight makes her an even more dangerous foe. Russia already has the means for prophesied aggression into the Middle East. She sits not far from the northern-most border of Iraq and Iran. Iran makes up ancient Persia, who will ally herself with Russia, Germany and others to finally come against the Antichrist, after he is situated in Israel. It certainly appears that Armaggedon is not far away.

There are many who believe that Russia will come down against Israel to fulfill the prophecies concerning Gog and Magog and that this will happen to begin the seven-year Tribulation. I don't see any reason from Scripture to believe this. The prophecy concerning Gog and Magog (Ezek. 38:17–20) is for the time of Jacob's trouble immediately following the Tribulation. Gog and Magog have long been identified with Russia by Christian and Jewish theologians, and Israel's religious scholars have long believed that when Russia descends on Israel, Messiah will come. We can see why when we look at this passage. Russia's descent on Israel will bring the wrath of God and the presence of the Lord to this earth, and as we have seen, that will not happen seven years prior to Christ's reign and the destruction of evil.

But the motive of the Russians to enter the Middle East will be two-fold—first, there is economic plight that can be cured by a takeover of the Middle East (Ezek. 38:13); second, the Antichrist system (whether the U.S. is included or not) will be increasing in power influence and aggressiveness in the Middle East (Dan.11:45). Russia will come down to confront the Antichrist system (Dan.11:40). As Russia and her allies move against the Middle East, God will dry up the Euphrates River and China will enter the conquest (Rev. 9:14; 16:12). All of this will transpire immediately after the tribulation of those days, and will create the time of Jacob's trouble, out of which one-third of Israel will be saved. Israel will repent and be received into the Church. The Rapture will occur and the Lord will destroy the Antichrist and his hordes at His coming.

What else might we expect?

In addition to these possibilities, there are other signs spoken of in Matthew chapter 24 which must occur. Here we see a great hatred for the saints in verse 9. We also see that the preaching of the gospel will reach throughout the entire world. The days preceding His return will involve great deception. False christs and false prophets will be present as the elect are looking for His return. Those false prophets will be saying, "Lo, he is in the wilderness," or "Lo, he is in the inner rooms." "But," the Lord says, "do not believe it." Then He tells us where we will meet Him. "Wherever the body is, there the eagles will be gathered together" (Matt. 24:26-28). We'll not meet Him in the inner room or in the wilderness, but in the air.

Among these false christs will be the New Age christs, those who have taken on their spirit guides. They will perform false wonders and lead many astray. Many in the ministry today have been initiated into the New Age. They have become these false christs. The New Age movement teaches that you and I will all become as Christ was when He was here. The New Age movement has one who is coming who will "show us all the way." That one is none other than the Antichrist.

Should you and I be looking for these things now, as I have thus far suggested? The answer is obviously yes, for God could put these events in motion at most any time. I can not promise you that these things will occur very soon, but I can tell you that the conditions are ripe, and things are occurring very rapidly. Consider the rapid decline of communism, the rapid coming together of the world against aggressors, and the increasing rapidity of earthquakes and catastrophic events. Perhaps this gives an excuse for those within the Church who have taught an imminent return. There are so many signs that are already fulfilled—the most obvious sign is of course the rebirth of the nation Israel.

What should we do to prepare?

Most dispensationalists teach that both Noah and Lot were a type of the Church removed from the wrath of God. On this point some who teach the pre-trib rapture are correct—for on the very day that Noah entered the ark, wrath came. And on the very day that Lot was removed from Sodom, God's wrath was poured out. The Rapture of the saints begins the 1,000-year day of God's wrath—the return of Christ to this earth to tread the winepress of God's wrath.

Although Lot and Noah were removed or protected, they knew what was going on around them. Both of these men were believers. Noah had worked hard and prepared as God had instructed him for the coming wrath. When it came, his obedience provided protection for both he and his family from the wrath of God. But what of Lot? Lot did nothing concerning the evil surrounding him. And when final judgment came, he was snatched away with his family. But the cost of his indifference was great, for he lost that which counted most to him in this life. He lost his beloved wife. Noah had prepared, Lot had not. When wrath came, Noah and his entire family were preserved through it. But what of Lot? After God's wrath had struck, Lot was found in mourning, and in a drunken stupor, having been defiled by his own daughters. Yes, the price of pleasure and procrastination is great.

A better account of the Church's resistance to Mystery Babylon is found in the account of Shadrach, Meshach, and Abednego. These men are a type of the last-days Church, which will be delivered out of the fire of persecution. They were not delivered from the fire, but were taken through the fire. The one who sentenced them was none other than the king of Babylon, from whence came the Mystery Religion. Why were they sentenced? Because they refused to worship this false god who demanded worship, and as such was a type of the Antichrist.

In our own century there have been those who have had to decide between Jesus and this world's goods. I remember a few years after I had come to know the Lord, I was sitting in a Full Gospel Businessmen's meeting and listening to two women speak. They had been smuggling Bibles behind the Iron Curtain into Eastern Europe. Sigi was a German Christian who had escaped from behind that same Iron Curtain. I remember almost as if it were yesterday how she explained her escape. She had left everything and fled with just the clothes on her back across the border. But, I also remember her telling of those who attempted to do the same, while clinging to their most precious earthly possessions. They did not make it. The extra weight of their worldly goods slowed them down, and they were shot as they struggled with those possessions.

What is it that might keep you from Jesus? I love my pre-tribulational and mid-tribulational brothers.

However, their message has not stirred the saints to preparedness. The problem with their teaching is this—it allows men to grow cold in their commitment and begin to live as Lot had done. Yet our times require a commitment similar to that of Noah. Noah realized that the ark must be completed, that the battle was not over until it was over.

God calls for endurance during the storms of life. The coming storm is certainly no exception. The fact that many within the Church will fall away in these days should instill in us additional motivation for endurance. Endurance means obedience to God's leading. The Holy Spirit's leading will always line up with God's Word. The confusion comes when we try to make the Word say something other than what it is clearly teaching. Are we preparing? It's never too late to make preparation. We are all a product of our decisions. Have we set our faces like a flint, as did the saints of old, even in the face of opposition? Or do we stand to lose everything, possibly our beloved and even our children, to the evils around us? The testing is sure to come, and even if it does not come in our day, our commitment must still be sure.

The early Church was prepared for persecution because they knew that it was coming. The Lord had told them. The apostles had told them. They had believed that they were in the midst of tribulation. They were. Yet, we still ignore the teachings of Scripture to be ready. Being ready requires preparedness. Our children need to know that these things are coming. They need to understand the reasons why, so that they can stand in the evil day. They need to be taught that God will honor their endurance, and provide grace in their hour of need. They need to understand that this world's goods will mean nothing in that day!

Final warning

What we have seen is based upon God's Word, and I do believe that God will honor His Word. Yet you may or may not have caught the message. You may still have other unanswered questions. You may be saying it could be this way or it could be that. And really what difference does it make? My brethren I ask you this: if I am wrong, so what? We will all be raptured prior to this time of great trouble, and the two-part coming theorists will be proven correct. But if what I have seen and presented to you here from Scripture is correct (and I believe with all of my being that it is), then are you prepared for what is coming? Or in your mind is God going to have let you down because you have wrongly believed that He will snatch you from trouble? Will you turn from Him and be yet another casualty of deception because you misunderstood God's Word? Or worse, will you watch as your children fail to understand and fall away, those for whom you would lay down your very life, if possible, to save? Many today sacrifice to send their children to the best college, and sacrifice to see that their child has the best in clothing and housing. Today, I am afraid that our people are too busy seeking the things of this world and the knowledge of this world, but neglect the weightier matters of life. God forgive us!

The Lord is coming, but I'm afraid that we are the ones not prepared this time. Israel *is* being prepared this time. Great understanding of Scripture is coming forth within the messianic Jewish community. My great fear is that this message will not change things, because most church members are weak in their love for and study of the Word. Our leadership is weak within the churches. Even where we have strong spiritual leadership, there is no urgency to prepare the people. There is a blindness to what is coming—just as there was a blindness within Israel at the time of Messiah's first coming. Pastors, the spiritual life of your people depends on preparedness. Fathers, the spiritual life of your family depends on their preparedness. Christ must be placed back as our Head. Repentance must come.

But, you say, if this is all true, how do I trust, how do I prepare? The major preparation is not physical. It is spiritual. If you have believed and repented of your sinful rebellious nature against God, having recognized that the price that the Lord Jesus Christ paid for your inclusion into the kingdom was sufficient to totally cleanse you, and having done this committed your life to the Lord, then you are sealed by His Spirit, born into His kingdom. The Holy Spirit has become your guide, and He is bearing witness with your spirit. Seek to walk with Him daily, being filled with Him always (putting off the old man and putting on the new). If you heed His witness you will grow stronger; but if you disobey His witness you will grow weaker, and as a result you will grow weaker in your commitment to Him.

Be alert to the voice of the Lord. He speaks through His Word to the inner man. "And your ears shall hear a word behind you, saying, 'This is the way, walk in it,' when you turn to the right or when you turn to the left" (Isa.30:21). Know and be true to the Bible, for His Word will allow you to be discerning of His voice. Be alert to the signs; He's coming soon, but before He comes there "shall be great tribulation such as the world has never seen, no, nor ever shall be. And except those days should be shortened, there should no flesh be saved: but for the elect's sake those days shall be shortened" (Matt. 24:21–22).

As you continue your Christian walk, remember these words of our Lord: "For whosoever will save his life shall lose it: and whosoever will lose his life for my sake shall find it"(Matt. 16:25). Also remember that He has promised to be with us "even to the end of the age"(Matt. 28:20b). Trust Him not yourself—for taking up your cross involves applying His cross to our lives daily. Always remember that He died for you that you might live for Him. He was raised for you, that you might live with Him in glory.

Maranatha, see you in the Kingdom.

Yours in Christ,

Jerry M. Parks

END NOTES

Chapter One

1. 1 Thess. 5:4. RSV
2. Rev. 12:12-17.
3. Dave Hunt, *Global Peace and the Rise of Antichrist* (Eugene, Oreg.: Harvest House Publishers, 1990), 145.
4. Ibid., 23.
5. See John 17:6-10 & 20.
6. Hal Lindsay, *The Road to Holocaust* (New York: Bantam Books, 1989), 282.
7. Norman Geisler, *False Gods of Our Time* (Eugene, Oreg.: Harvest House Publishers, 1985), 81. Pantheism is the belief in the false god of nature, where the universe is all that there is. God is seen as eminent or in everything and everyone.
8. Grant Jeffrey, *Armageddon: Appointment with Destiny* (New York: Bantam Books, 1988), 163.
9. Ibid., 161.
10. Dave Hunt, *Global Peace and the Rise of Antichrist* (Eugene, Oreg.: Harvest House Publishers, 1990), 26.
11. Lindsay, *The Road to Holocaust*, 269.
12. Ibid.

Notes

Chapter Two

1. Grant Jeffrey, *Armageddon: Appointment with Destiny* (New York: Bantam Books, 1988), 134.
2. Dave Hunt, *Global Peace and the Rise of Antichrist* (Eugene, Oreg.: Harvest House Publishers, 1990), 28.
3. Ibid., 217.

Chapter Three

1. Hal Lindsay with C.C. Carlson, *The Late Great Planet Earth* (Grand Rapids, Mich.: Zondervan Publishing House, 1970), 129-130
2. Ibid., 130.
3. H.L. Dr. Willmington, *Willmington's Guide to the Bible* (Wheaton, Ill.: Tyndale House, 1981), 76.

Chapter Four

1. Num. 16:42-48.
2. Eph. 2:3.
3. 2 Thess. 1:7b-9.
4. Rev. 12:12.
5. Dan. 12:7b.
6. John F. Walvoord and Roy B. Zuck, *The Bible Knowledge Commentary–New Testament Edition* (Wheaton, Ill.: Victor Books, a Division of SP Publications, Inc., 1983), 484.
7. 1 Cor. 15:51-52a.
8. Russell Chandler, *Understanding the New Age* (Dallas: Word Publishers, 1991), 78.

Chapter Five

1. Henry Clarence Thiessen, *Lectures in Systematic Theology* (Grand Rapids: Wm. B. Erdman Publishing Co., 1979), 375.

2. John F. Walvoord and Roy B. Zuck, *The Bible Knowledge Commentary–New Testament Edition* (Wheaton, Ill.: Victor Books a Division of SP Publications, Inc., 1983), 719.

3. David Lurie Ph.D., *The Covenant, the Holocaust and the Seventieth Week.* (Coral Gables, Fla., 2d printing: Messianic Century, 1989), 100.

4. Marvin Rosenthal, *The Pre-Wrath Rapture of the Church* (Nashville: Thomas Nelson Publishers, 1990), 257. (Reference Dan. 10:12-13 and 21; Dan. 12:1-2; and Rev. 12:7)

5. David Ellis, "Gorby: The New Age Guru" *Time Magazine*, vol. 135, No. 25 (18 June 1990): 15.

6. A quote of former President Jimmy Carter, *The News & Daily Advance*, Lynchburg, Va. (Sat., 20 July 1990: B-8.

7. Texe Marrs *Dark Secrets of the New Age* (Westchester, Ill.: Crossway Books–a Division of Good News Publishers, 1987), 169. (Referencing–Lola Davis, *Toward A World Religion for the New Age* [New York: Coleman Publishing, 1983], 13.)

Chapter Six

1. Walter Tuck Parkerson, MD., *Israel Behold Your God*, Self-Published, copyright TXU 287490, 1987., 51-54.

2. Grant Jeffrey, *Armageddon: Appointment with Destiny* (New York: Bantam Books, 1988), 133.

3. Ibid., 133-4.

4. Ibid., Jeffrey relates this to Paul's crown of righteousness in 2 Tim. 4:8; 2 Cor. 5:10 is also referenced.

5. Ibid., 135-7.

6. Ibid., 137-9, Jeffrey also references Rev. 6:17 and 7:1-8 in his argument.

7. Millard J. Erickson, *Contemporary Options in Eschatology–A Study of the Millennium* 5th printing (Grand Rapids, Mich.: Baker Book House, 1977–1985), 130.

8. Ibid., 131-32, Erickson also references Ladd, *The Blessed Hope*, 20, 37, 41, 43. in his argument.

9. Dave MacPherson, *The Unbelievable Pre-trib Origin* (Kansas City, Mo.: Heart of America Bible Society, 1973), 94.

10. Ibid., 47.

11. Oliver B. Greene, *The Epistle of the Apostle Paul to the Thessalonians* (Greenville, S.C.: The Gospel Hour Inc., 1964), 153-54.

12. John F. Walvoord and Roy B. Zuck, *The Bible Knowledge Commentary–New Testament Edition* (Wheaton, Ill.: Victor Books a Division of SP Publications, Inc., 1983), 79.

13. Oliver B. Greene, *Bible Truth* (Greenville, S. C.: The Gospel Hour Inc., 1968), 367-68.

14. Ibid., 369.

Chapter Seven

1. Hal Lindsay with C.C. Carlson, *The Late Great Planet Earth* (Grand Rapids, Mich.: Zondervan Publishing House, 1970), 162.

2. Ibid., 99.

3. Robert L. Saucy, *The Church in God's Program* (Chicago: The Moody Bible Institute, 1972), 12.

4. Ibid., 13.

5. Ibid.

6. Ibid.

7. Ibid., 13 & 15.

8. Ibid., 17.

9. Now, before we proceed with Paul's use of the word "elect," I should point out that most dispensationalists see this word "elect," in Matthew 24, as being representative of the nation Israel. (Although, some say that the elect spoken of here are the saved of the Great Tribulation.)

10. 2 Tim. 2:10.

11. Grant Jeffrey, *Armageddon: Appointment with Destiny* (New York: Bantam Books, 1988), 135.

Chapter Eight

1. Dave Hunt, *Global Peace and the Rise of Antichrist* (Eugene, Oreg.: Harvest House Publishers, 1990), 202.

2. Ibid.

3. Ibid., 193 & 198.

4. Ibid., 279.

5. Grant Jeffrey, *Armageddon: Appointment with Destiny* (New York: Bantam Books, 1988), 171.

6. Ibid., 34-43.

7. Oliver B. Greene, *Bible Truth* (Greenville, S.C.: The Gospel Hour Inc., 1968), 371.

8. John F. Walvoord and Roy B. Zuck, *The Bible Knowledge Commentary—New Testament Edition* (Wheaton, Ill.: Victor Books, a Division of SP Publications, Inc., 1983), 717.

9. Millard J. Erickson, *Contemporary Options in Eschatology—A Study of the Millennium* 5th printing (Grand Rapids, Mich.: Baker Book House, 1977—1985), 141.

10. John 20:18-19.

Chapter Nine

1. Robert H. Gundry, *The Church and the Tribulation* (Grand Rapids: Zondervan Publishing House, 1973), 56-59, as quoted by : Millard J. Erickson, *Contemporary Options in Eschatology–A Study of the Millennium* (Grand Rapids, Mich.: Baker Book House, 1977—fifth printing 1985), 154.

2. Ibid.

3. Ibid., 154-55.

4. Ibid., 155.

Chapter Ten

1. Dave Hunt, *Global Peace and the Rise of Antichrist* (Eugene, Oreg.: Harvest House Publishers, 1990), 216.

2. Louis Sperry Chafer, *Systematic Theology*, Vol. 4 (Dallas: Dallas Seminary Press, 1948), 398

3. Daniel 9:24 tells us that Israel will see an end to "iniquity" and that this week will "bring in everlasting righteousness" for Israel confirming their salvation prior to its end.

4. Judah J. Slotkil, *Daniel, Ezra, Nehemiah* (London: The Soncino Press, 1978), 101 (Referenced by Marvin Rosenthal, *The Pre-Wrath Rapture of the Church* (Nashville: Thomas Nelson Publishers, 1990), 258.

5. Marvin Rosenthal, *The Pre-Wrath Rapture of the Church* (Nashville: Thomas Nelson Publishers, 1990), 258.

6. See 2 Peter 3:8-10, and compare with Luke 13:32, Psm. 90:4, and Hos. 5:15-6:2. A day unto the Lord is as 1000 years.

7. Eph. 2:12-15; Heb. 8:1-13.

8. Joseph Good, *Rosh HaShanah and the Messianic Kingdom to Come* (Port Arthur, Tex.: Hatikva Ministries, 1989), 131 (References: Kieval Herman, *The*

High Holy Days [New York: The Burning Bush Press, 1959], 120.

9. Ibid., 42-43.

10. Ibid., 43.

11. Ibid., 89-90.

12. Ibid., 90.

13. John F. Walvoord and Roy B. Zuck, *The Bible Knowledge Commentary–New Testament Edition* (Wheaton, Ill.: Victor Books a Division of SP Publications, Inc., 1983), 957.

14. Henry Clarence Thiessen, *Lectures in Systematic Theology* (Grand Rapids, Mich.: Wm. B. Erdman Publishing Co., 1979), 387-394.

15. Ibid., 375.

Chapter Eleven

1. Dave Hunt, *Global Peace and the Rise of Antichrist* (Eugene, Oreg.: Harvest House Publishers, 1990), 31.

2. Randall Baer, *Inside the New Age Nightmare* (Lafayette, La.: Huntington House Publishers, 1989), 182.

3. Lola Davis, *Toward a World Religion for the New Age* (Farmingdale, N.Y.: Coleman Publishing, 1983), 189.

4. Ibid., 180.

5. Frank R. Wallace, Interviewed by NTP Columnist Eric Savage, *NTP News Report* (Henderson, Nev.: Neo-Tech Publishing Company, 1990), 10.

6. Ibid., 16.

7. Norman Geisler Ph.D., *The Seductive Embrace of the New Age Movement* (Lynchbury: Quest Productions, 1989), quote taken from taped message.

8. Ibid., *The Christian Response to the New Age Movement* .

Chapter Twelve

1. Henry Clarence Thiessen, *Lectures in Systematic Theology* (Grand Rapids, Mich.: Wm. B. Erdman Publishing Co., 1979), 201.

2. Michael Horton, ed., *The Agony of Deceit* (Chicago, Ill.: Moody Press, 1990), 13.

3. Aaron Luther Pluger, *Things to Come for Planet Earth* (St. Louis, Mo.: Concordia Publishing House, 1977), 96.

4. Dave MacPherson, *The Unbelievable Pre-trib Origin* (Kansas City: Heart of America Bible Society, 1973), 104.

Chapter Thirteen

1. Hal Lindsay, *The Road to Holocaust* (New York: Bantam Books, 1989), 282.

2. Henry Steele Commager, *Jefferson, Nationalism, and the Enlightenment* (New York: George Brazeller, Inc., 1975), 125-139.

3. Ibid., 135-135.

4. David Wilkerson, *Set the Trumpet to Thy Mouth* (Lindale, Tex.: World Challenge, Inc., 1985), 25.

DEFINITIONS OF TERMS USED IN THIS BOOK

Amillennialist-
One who believes in a spiritualized millennium taking place during the Church age. He does not believe in the 1000-year reign of the Lord Jesus on this earth (see definition for "millennium").

Antichrist-
The Antichrist is the incarnation of Satan into a man who will attempt to control the world during the Great Tribulation. Antichrist is also the spirit opposed to Christ, His gospel, and His people.

Dominion Theology-
A sister theology of the Reconstructionist movement. The Dominionists are mainly coming from Pentecostal and Charismatic circles. This is a minority movement within these groups. Dominionists are mainly "name it and claim it" preachers (also see Reconstructionist).

Great Tribulation-
A period thought to be 7 years long, during which the Antichrist will rule over the world amid unification of religion and government. Also a time of transformation from this present age dominated by gentile rule, and the coming kingdom in which Christ will physically rule the earth with a rod of iron.

Definitions

Mid-Tribulationist-

One who sees the Rapture of the Church in the middle of the Tribulation.

Millennium-

The 1000-year period of time recorded in Scripture, during which Christ will rule with a rod of iron over all gentile nations. A time when sacrifice will be reintroduced to cover the sin of the unsaved.

New Age-

The present day revival of Mystery Babylon promising a more perfect world as mankind evolves into the Aquarian Age. An age when men will become as christs or gods; when all negativism and separatism will vanish from off the earth; where man works in cooperation with the god, who is the universe of which man is a part. A movement which Christians see as the system of the Antichrist.

Partial rapture Theory-

Those who see only the Spirit-baptized church as being raptured. The lukewarm church will remain through the Tribulation.

Post-millennialist-

One who believes that there will be a millennium of unknown duration occurring as an age of peace on earth brought on by the spread of Christian doctrine. However, it will not be literally ruled from earth by Christ. Instead, He will rule through the Church. The Millennium therefore will be followed by the Second Coming of Christ for His saints to set up the heavenly kingdom.

Definitions

Post-tribulationalist-

One who believes that Christ will return after the Great Tribulation and that the Rapture of the Church will take place in conjunction with, but immediately before, that earthly return.

Pre-millennialist-

One who sees the Second Coming of Christ occurring prior to the Millennium.

Pre-tribulationalist-

One who sees the Rapture as occurring before the Tribulation, and the Second Coming as occurring in two stages known as the Rapture and the revelation.

Rapture-

The catching away of believers from the face of the earth. This will occur immediately after the resurrection of the dead in Christ. To the Pre-tribulationalist, this is the first stage of the Second Coming.

Reconstructionist Theology-

A theological position which is an outgrowth of Post-millennialism. The teaching is that the Church has replaced Israel, and that the Church will bring about a period of peace known as the Millennium prior to the return of the Lord Jesus.

Resurrection-

1. The first resurrection of the dead is for all those who are in Christ. This occurs before the Millennium.

2. The second resurrection of the dead is for all those outside of Christ. This occurs immediately at the end of the Millennium.

Definitions

Revelation of Jesus Christ-

This is not the book of Revelation, but the actual appearing of and return to the earth by the Lord Jesus Christ. This is the term coined by theologians to mean the physical earthly return. In the two-part coming theories this is the second stage of the Second Coming.

Second Coming of the Lord Jesus Christ-

The literal physical appearing of Christ.

Bibliography

Alder, Vera. *When Humanity Comes of Age*. New York: Samuel Weiser, 1974.

Bailey, Alice. "Djwhal Khul—Food for Thought." n.p.

Bailey, Alice. *The Rays and the Initiations*. New York: Lucis Publishing Co., 1982.

Baer, Randall. *Inside the New Age Nightmare*. Lafayette, La.: Huntington House, 1989.

Chafer, Louis Sperry. *Systematic Theology*. Vol. 4, Dallas: Seminary Press, 1948.

Chandler, Russell. *Understanding the New Age*. Dallas: Word Publishers, 1991.

Commager, Henry Steele. *Jefferson, Nationalism and the Enlightenment*. New York: George Brazeller, Inc., 1975.

Cumbey, Constance. *A Planned Deception The Staging of a New Age Messiah*. East Detroit, Mich.: Pointe Publishers, 1985.

Cumbey, Constance. *Hidden Dangers of the Rainbow*. Lafayette, La.: Huntington House, 1983.

Davis, Lola. *Toward a World Religion for the New Age*. Farmingdale. N.Y.: Coleman Publishing, 1983.

Bibliography

Ellis, David. "Gorby: The New Age Guru." *Time magazine*, Vol. 135, No. 25 (18 June 1990): 15.

Erickson, Millard J. *Contemporary Options in Eschatology—A Study of the Millennium*. Grand Rapids: Baker Book House, 1985.

Falwell, Jerry. *Liberty Bible Commentary New Testament*. Nashville: Thomas Nelson, 1982.

Geisler, Norman. *False Gods of Our Time*, Eugene Oreg.: Harvest House Publishers, 1985.

Good, Joseph. *Rosh HaShanah and the Messianic Kingdom to Come*. Port Arthur, Tex.: Hatikva Ministries, 1989.

Greene, Oliver B. *Bible Truth*. Greenville, S.C.: The Gospel Hour, Inc., 1968.

Greene, Oliver B. *Daniel*. Greenville, S.C.: The Gospel Hour, Inc., 1964.

Greene, Oliver B. *The Epistle of the Apostle Paul to the Thessalonians*. Greenville, S.C.: The Gospel Hour, Inc., 1964.

Greene, Oliver B. *The Epistle of the Apostle Paul to the Ephesians*. Greenville, S.C.: The Gospel Hour, Inc., 1963.

Greene, Oliver B. *The Revelation Verse by Verse Study*. Greenville, S.C.: The Gospel Hour, Inc., 1963.

Gundry, Robert H. *The Church and the Tribulation*. Grand Rapids: Zondervan Publishing House, 1973.

Bibliography

Gundry, Robert H. *The Tribulation*. (As quoted by Millard J. Erickson in *Contemporary Options in Eschatology*. Grand Rapids: Baker Book House, 1985.)

Herman, Kieval. *The High Holy Days*. New York: The Burning Bush Press, 1959.

Hone, William. *The Apocryphal New Testament*. Lindgate Hill, London: n.p., 1820.

Horton, Michael. ed. *The Agony of Deceit*. Chicago: Moody Press, 1990.

Hunt, Dave. *Global Peace and the Rise of Antichrist*. Eugene, Oreg.: Harvest House Publishers, 1990.

Jefferson, Thomas. *The Jefferson Bible*. Boston: Beacon Press, 1989.

Jeffery, Grant. *Armageddon: Appointment with Destiny*. New York: Bantam Books, 1988.

Jeffery, Grant R. *Heaven the Last Frontier*. Toronto, Ontario: Frontier Research Publication, 1990.

Kah, Gary H. *En Route to Global Occupation*. Lafayette, La.: Huntington House Publishers, 1992.

Keys, Ken Jr. *Handbook to Higher Consciousness*. Coos Bay, Oreg.: Love Line Book, 1975.

Lemesurier, Peter. *The Armageddon Script*. New York: St. Martin's Press, 1981.

Lindsay, Hal with C.C. Carlson. *The Late Great Planet Earth*. Grand Rapids, Mich.: Zondervan Publishing House, 1970.

Bibliography

Lindsay, Hal. *The Road to Holocaust*. New York: Bantam Books, 1989.

Lurie, David Ph.D. *The Covenant the Holocaust and the Seventieth Week*. Coral Gables, Fla.: Messianic Century, 1989.

MacPherson, Dave. *The Unbelievable Pretrib Origin*. Kansas City, Mo.: Heart of America Bible Society, 1973.

Marrs, Texe. *Dark Secrets of the New Age*. Westchester, Ill.: Crossway Books—a Division of Good News Publishers, 1987.

Marrs, Texe. *Millennium*. Austin, Tex.: Living Truth Publishers, 1990.

Martin, Walter. *The Kingdom of the Cults*. Minneapolis: Bethany House, 1985.

Moffat, James. "The Revelation of St. John the Divine." (in Vol. V of *The Expositor's Greek Testament*, W. Robert Nicoll, ed, Grand Rapids: Wm. B. Erdmans Publishing Co., 1977.)

Mounce, Robert H. *The Book of Revelation*. (in New International Commentary on the New Testament) Grand Rapids: Wm. B. Erdmans Publishing Co., 1977.

Murray, Iain H. *The Puritan Hope, Revival and the Interpretation of Prophecy*. Edinburgh: Banner of Truth Trust, 1971.

Pluger, Aaron Luther. *Things to Come for Planet Earth*. St. Louis: Concordia Publishing House, 1977.

Bibliography

Parkerson, Walter Tuck MD. *Israel Behold Your God.* n.p.: Self-Published, 1987.

Peck, Scott M. *New Age Journal.* (May-June 1987): 51.

Rosenthal, Marvin. *The Pre-Wrath Rapture of the Church.* Nashville: Thomas Nelson Publishers, 1990.

Saucy, Robert L. *The Church in God's Program.* Chicago: The Moody Bible Institute of Chicago, 1972.

Scofield, C. I. *The Scofield Reference Bible.* New York: Oxford University Press, 1909.

Thiessen, Henry Clarence. *Lectures in Systematic Theology.* Grand Rapids: Wm. B. Erdman Publishing Co., 1979.

Walvoord, John F. and Roy B. Zuck—editors. *The Bible Knowledge Commentary—New Testament Edition.* Wheaton, Ill.: Victor Books, 1983.

Walvoord, John F. *The Rapture Question.* Findlay, Ohio: Dunham, 1957.

Wilkerson, David. *Set the Trumpet to Thy Mouth.* Lindale, Tex.: World Challenge, Inc., 1985.

Willimington, H. L. Dr., *Willmington's Guide to the Bible.* Wheaton, Ill.: Tyndale House Publishers, 1986.

* * * *

Against Heresies 10.4, trans, A. Roberts and J. Donaldson, in *The Anti-nicene Fathers*, ed. Roberts and Donaldson, 10 vols. Buffalo Christian Lit., 1895-96, 1:560.

Bibliography

Author not listed, *Revelation Its Grand Climax at Hand!*, New York: Watchtower Bible and Track Society of New York, Inc., 1988.

Harper Study Bible/Holy Bible—Revised Standard Version. Grand Rapids: Zondervan Publishing House. O.T. 1952/N.T. 1972, used in all scriptural quotes unless otherwise noted.

MORE GOOD BOOKS FROM HUNTINGTON HOUSE PUBLISHERS

RECENT RELEASES

America: Awaiting the Verdict
by Mike Fuselier

We are a nation stricken with an infectious disease. The disease is called betrayal—we are a nation that has denied, rejected, and betrayed our Christian past. The symptoms of the disease are many and multiplying daily. Mike Fuselier thus encourages Americans to return to the faith of their founding fathers—the faith upon which our law and government rest—or suffer the consequences. To prove that our forebearers were in no way attempting to establish a secular state, as contended by secular humanists, the author presents oft-forgotten but crucial evidence to fortify his—and all Christians'—case.

ISBN 1-56384-034-0 $5.99

Battle Plan: Equipping the Church for the 90s
by Chris Stanton

Already into the nineties and it's easy to see that the institutions of American society—the family, the church, the government—will continue to look little like the same entities of all prior decades! The evidences have been discussed before. Now is the time to talk about why and what to do about it. A new battle plan is needed. The author dissects the characteristics of the enemy and the effectiveness of its attacks on the church. Then he lays out the military strategy for the spiritual warriors of the 1990s. The enemy won't know what hit him if the Church diligently readies itself for this all-important battle!

ISBN 1-56384-034-0 $7.99

The Blessings of Liberty: Restoring the City on the Hill
by Charles Heath

The author believes Liberalism is destroying our nation. If we continue to do nothing, says Heath, the traditional family values that we cherish and the kind of government envisioned by our founding fathers will cease to exist. Heath presents a coherent case for limited government, decentralized and self-governing communities, and a return to traditional values. Conservatism, he continues, has its premise in the book of Genesis. It is the only viable philosophy capable of addressing and solving today's problems.

ISBN 1-56384-005-7 $8.99

Don't Touch That Dial:
The Impact of the Media on Children and the Family
by Barbara Hattemer & Robert Showers

Men and women without any stake in the outcome of the war between the pornographers and our families have come to the qualified, professional agreement that media does have an effect on our children—an effect that is devastatingly, significant. Highly respected researchers, psychologists, and sociologists join the realm of pediatricians, district attorneys, parents, teachers, pastors, and community leaders—who have diligently remained true to the fight against filthy media—in their latest comprehensive critique of the modern media establishment (i.e., film, television, print, art).

ISBN Quality Trade Paper   1-56384-032-4 $9.99
ISBN Hardcover 1-56384-035-9 $19.99

En Route to Global Occupation
by Gary Kah

High-ranking government liaison Gary Kah warns that national sovereignty will soon be a thing of the past. Invited to join the WCPA (World Constitution and Parliamentary Association), the author was involved in the planning and implementation of a one-world government. For the skeptical observer, the material in this book "should serve as ample evidence that the drive to create a one-world government is for real." Reproductions of the original documentation are included.

ISBN   0-910311-97-8 $9.99

Face the Wind
by Gloria Delaney

Thoughts of suicide, abuse, rape, drugs, booze, tattoos, jail, anger, hatred, revenge, and depression marked the endless cycle of the author's life as Speedy, an unloved teen-ager and "motorcycle old lady"; she was the possession of Crazy Nick. When she discovered that she was pregnant and felt the baby first move within her, panic turned to determination. Little Michael was born, and, through the vile corruption of life with Crazy, Gloria clung to the beauty of motherhood and the innocence of her child, committing herself to his welfare above all else. Read about her escape with Michael and how she found the One who would lift her out of her past and make her wholly clean. This book celebrates motherhood and demonstrates how the miracle of new life can point the lost to the Author of Life.

ISBN 1-56384-011-1 $9.99

False Security:
Has the New Age Given Us a False Hope?
by Jerry Parks

The Great Tribulation! Wars, famine, pestilence, persecution—these are just some of the frightful events in the future of the world. Are they in your future? For centuries, the prophets searched the Scriptures for the timing of the first coming of the Messiah, now we watch and wait for the Second Coming of Christ and everything that foreshadows it. In *False Security: Has the New Age Given Us a False Hope?* author Jerry Parks discusses a relatively recent teaching that has infiltrated the Church, giving many a false hope. When will the Rapture occur? Be prepared to examine your own beliefs and clear up many of the questions you may have about the close of this age.

ISBN 1-56384-012-X $9.99

Hitler and the New Age
by Bob Rosio

Hail Caesar! Heil Hitler! Hail —who? Who will be next? Many recognize Caesar and Nero and Hitler as forerunners of the future, when one leader, backed by one government and religious church, will lead one worldwide system. The question is, Were they all tools to prepare the way for the very old and evil world order? Bob Rosio believes that studying an extreme type of historical figure, such as Hitler, will help Christians better understand and better prepare a battle plan to stand against the New Age movement and this emerging world order. He describes this book as "a study in the mechanics of evil."

ISBN 1-56384-009-X $9.99

Journey into Darkness: Nowhere to Land
by Stephen L. Arrington

This story begins on Hawaii's glistening sands and ends in the mysterious deep of the Great White Shark. In between he found himself trapped in the drug smuggling trade—unwittingly becoming the "Fall Guy" in the highly publicized John Z. DeLorean drug case. Naval career shattered, his youthful innocence tested, and friends and family put to the test of loyalty, Arrington locked on one Truth during his savage stay in prison and endeavors to share that critical truth now. Focusing on a single important message to young people—to stay away from drugs—the author recounts his horrifying prison experience and allows the reader to take a peek at the source of hope and courage that helped him survive.

ISBN 1-56384-003-3 $9.99

A Jewish Conservative Looks at Pagan America
by Don Feder

With eloquence and insight that rival essayists of antiquity, Don Feder's pen finds his targets in the enemies of God, family, and American tradition and morality. Deftly...delightfully...the master allegorist and Titian with a typewriter brings clarity to the most complex sociological issues and invokes giggles and wry smiles from both followers and foes. Feder is Jewish to the core, and he finds in his Judaism no inconsistency with an American Judeo-Christian ethic. Questions of morality plague school administrators, district court judges, senators, congressmen, parents, and employers; they are wrestling for answers in a "changing world." But Feder challenges the evolving society theory and directs inquirers to the original books of wisdom: the Torah and the Bible.

ISBN Quality Trade Paper 1-56384-036-7 $9.99
ISBN Hardcover 1-56384-037-5 $19.99

Political Correctness:
The Cloning of the American Mind
by David Thibodaux, Ph.D.

The author, professor of literature at the University of Southwestern Louisiana, confronts head on the movement that is now being called Political Correctness. Political correctness, says Thibodaux, "is an umbrella under which advocates of civil rights, gay and lesbian rights, feminism, and environmental causes have gathered." To incur the wrath of these groups, one only has to disagree with them on political, moral, or social issues. To express traditionally Western concepts in universities today can result in not only ostracism, but even suspension. (According to a recent "McNeil-Lehrer News Hour" report, one student was suspended for discussing the reality of the moral law with an avowed homosexual. He was reinstated only after he apologized.)

ISBN Quality Trade Paper 1-56384-026-X $9.99
ISBN Hardcover 1-56384-033-2 $18.99

One Year to a College Degree
by Lynette Long & Eileen Hershberger

College—Anyone who's been through the gauntlet of higher education's administrative red tape can attest to the frustration and confusion that accompanies the process. Twenty-eight years after a failed first semester, co-author Eileen Hershberger embarked on the admirable, albeit frightening, venture as an adult learner. One year later she earned her bachelor's degree. With Lynette Long, she reveals the secret in this thorough self-help book, complete with reference guide, work sheets, and resource lists. Most intriguing are the inside tips only professors and upper-level counselors would know.

ISBN 1-56384-001-4 $9.99

The Subtle Serpent: New Age in the Classroom
by Darylann Whitemarsh &
Bill Reisman

There is a new morality being taught to our children in public schools. Without the consent or even awareness of parents—educators and social engineers are aggressively introducing new moral codes to our children. In most instances, the new moral codes contradict the traditional values. Darylann Whitemarsh (1989 Teacher of the Year) and Bill Reisman (educator and expert on the occult) combine their knowledge to expose the deliberate madness occurring in our public schools.

ISBN 1-56384-016-2 $9.99

Touching the Face of God
by Bob Russell

This book chronicles the spiritual odyssey of Bob Russell—author, pilot, super-salesman, Christian philosopher. It is the gripping account of one man's love affair with the sky and the obstacles he overcame to become one of America's best-known aviators. It is also the story of how he reaffirmed his faith in everything he did—and how his courage helped him to survive the heartbreaking loss of friends, children, and wife. The author notes his life from the Great Depression until the twilight of the Cold War. It is a true account of survival in the face of poverty and war and an intimate picture of love and marriage.

ISBN Quality Trade Paper 1-56384-010-3 $8.99

When the Wicked Seize a City
by Chuck & Donna McIlhenny with Frank York
A highly publicized lawsuit . . . a house fire-bombed in the night
. . . the shatter of windows smashed by politically (and wickedly)
motivated vandals cuts into the night . . . All because Chuck
McIlhenny voiced God's condemnation of a behavior and life-style
and protested the destruction of society that results from its practice.
That behavior is homosexuality, and that life-style is the gay culture.
This book explores: the rise of gay power and what it will mean if
Christians do not organize and prepare for the battle; homosexual
attempts to have the American Psychiatric Association remove
pedophilia from the list of mental illnesses—now they want
homophobia declared a disorder.

ISBN 1-56384-024-3 $9.99

You Hit Like a Girl
by Elsa Houtz & William J. Ferkile
Rape—it's the issue that dominates the headlines. Have things
changed since the days when women and children were afforded
respect and care by all members of society? What does self-protection
mean in the 1990s in this age of higher rates of violent crime and the
"progressiveness" of the women's movement? What can women do
to protect themselves? What can men do to protect the women they
love—or the children they'd sacrifice their very lives to shelter from
harm? The authors, self-defense experts, have developed a thorough
guide to self-protection that addresses the mental attitude of
common sense safety and details the practical means by which
women can protect themselves and their children.

ISBN 1-56384-031-6 $9.99

NOVELS

Angel Vision
by Jim Carroll & Jay Gaines

Legends about the mysterious and beautiful Ozark mountains in Arkansas abound among the locals. Three men, strangers to one another, find themselves pitted against the evil housed deep within the Lost Louisiana Mine. Millionaire Walter Carson, Reverend Victor Peterson, and karate instructor Jason Howser are involved in separate accidents that leave each of them in a deep coma. Neither dead nor alive, the three awaken to meet their ghostly comrades and a mysterious stranger, Clay, who attempts to fuse them into a team of survivors and warriors for the Lord.

ISBN Mass Market Paperback 1-56384-006-5 $5.99

Legend of the Holy Lance
by Bill Still

From an awesome galactic rock, the most mysterious weapons in history will be forged: The Holy Lance and Sword. These icons of power will become the symbols of conquerors: Saul, Nebuchadnezzar, Cyrus the Persian, Alexander the Great, Julius Caesar, Constantine, Attila the Hun, Merlin, Napoleon, and Hitler. The Lance was ensconced in museums, hidden in ice caves and castle walls, and raised to the status of holy relic as the purported spear that pierced the side of Christ. A career-hardened reporter and a beautiful Yale senior discover that the Lance is held by a secret society in Germany and find themselves catapulted into the realm of international conspiracy.

ISBN Quality Trade Paper 1-56384-002-2 $8.99
ISBN Hardcover 1-56384-008-1 $16.99

Cover of Darkness
by J. Carroll

Jack's time is running out. The network's top investigative reporter has been given the most bizarre and difficult assignment of his life. The powers behind a grand conspiracy (occult and demonic forces) are finally exposed by Jack. Now comes the real challenge—convincing others. Matching wits with supernatural forces, Jack faces the most hideous conspiracy the world has ever known.

ISBN 0-910311-31-5 $7.99

Crystalline
Connection
by Bob Maddux &
Mary Carpenter Reid

Enter the enchanting world of Ebbern, a planet in many ways like our own. In the *Crystalline Connection*, our hero, Bracken, returns to his homeland after ten year of wandering. Once there he becomes involved in a monumental struggle, gallantly confronting the dark forces of evil. This futuristic fantasy is fraught with intrigue, adventure, romance and much more. The *Crystalline Connection* artfully discloses the devastating consequences of involvement in the New Age movement while using the medium of fiction.

ISBN 0-910311-71-4 $8.99

THE SALT SERIES

Exposing the AIDS Scandal
by Paul Cameron, M.D.

AIDS is 100 percent fatal all of the time. There are believed to be over 1,500,000 people in the United States carrying the AIDS virus. The ever-growing number of cases compels us to question whether there will be a civilization in twenty years.

ISBN 1-56384-023-5 $2.99

Inside the New Age Nightmare
by Randall Baer

Are your children safe from the New Age movement? This former New Age leader, one of the world's foremost experts in crystals, brings to light the darkest of the darkness that surrounds the New Age movement. The week that Randall Baer's original book was released, he met with a puzzling and untimely death—his car ran off a mountain pass. His death is still regarded as suspicious.

ISBN 1-56384-022-7 $2.99

The Question of Freemasonry
by Ed Decker

Blood oaths, blasphemy, and illegal activity—in this day and age it's hard to believe these aberrations still exist; this booklet demonstrates that the Freemasons are not simply a "goodwill" community-oriented organization.

ISBN 1-56384-020-0 $2.99

To Moroni with Love
by Ed Decker

Readers are led through the deepest of the Mormon church doctrines and encouraged to honestly determine whether the words can be construed as heresy in light of the true, unadulterated language of the Bible. Decker reveals shocking material that has caused countless Mormons to question the church leaders and abandon Mormonism's false teachings.

ISBN 1-56384-021-9 $2.99

America Betrayed
by Marlin Maddoux

This hard-hitting book exposes the forces in our country which seek to destroy the family, the schools, our culture, and our values. The author details exactly how the news media manipulates your mind. Maddoux is the host of the popular national radio talk show, "Point of View."

ISBN 0-910311-18-8 $6.99

Deadly Deception
by Jim Shaw & Tom McKinney

For the first time the 33d degree ritual is made public! Learn of the "secrets" and "deceptions" that are practiced daily around the world. Find out why Freemasonry teaches that it is the true religion, that all other religions are but corrupted and perverted forms of Freemasonry. If you know anyone in the Masonic movement, you must read this book.

ISBN 0-910311-54-4 $7.99

Delicate Balance
by John Zajac

Find out what forces in the universe are at work and why the earth is in a very delicate balance. The author displays his research to present the overall picture at hand that packages and interconnects economics, prophesy, ecology, militarism, and theology. Can modern science unlock the mysteries of the future? Can we determine our own fate or are we part of a larger scheme beyond our control?

ISBN 0-910311-57-9 $8.99

The Devil's Web
by Pat Pulling with Kathy Cawthon
This explosive exposé presents the first comprehensive guide to childhood and adolescent occult involvement. Written by a nationally recognized occult crime expert, the author explains how the violent occult underworld operates and how they stalk and recruit our children, teen-agers, and young adults for their evil purposes.

ISBN 0-910311-59-5 $8.99 Trade paper
ISBN 0-910311-63-3 $16.99 Hardcover

Dinosaurs and the Bible
by David W. Unfred
Every reader, young and old, will be fascinated by this ever-mysterious topic—exactly what happened to the dinosaurs? Author David Unfred draws a very descriptive picture of the history and fate of the dinosaurs, using the Bible as a reference guide. Does the Bible mention dinosaurs? What happened to dinosaurs, or are there some still living awaiting discovery?

ISBN 0-910311-70-6 $12.99 Hardcover

Devil Take the Youngest
by Winkie Pratney
A history of Satan's hatred of innocence and his historical treachery against the young. Pratney begins his journey in ancient Babylon and continues through to modern-day America where infants are murdered daily and children are increasingly victimized through pornography, prostitution, and humanism.

ISBN 0-910311-29-3 $8.99

From Rock to Rock
by Eric Barger
Over three years in the making, the pages of this book represent thousands of hours of detailed research as well as over twenty-six years of personal experience and study. The author presents a detailed study on many current rock entertainers, rock concerts, videos, lyrics, and occult symbols used within the industry. He also presents a rating system of over fifteen hundred past and present rock groups and artists.

ISNB 0-910311-61-7

Exposing the AIDS Scandal
by Dr. Paul Cameron
Where do you turn when those who control the flow of information in this country withhold the truth? Why is the national media hiding facts from the public? Can AIDS be spread in ways we're not being told? Finally, a book that gives you a total account for the AIDS epidemic, and what steps can be taken to protect yourself. What you don't know can kill you!

ISBN 0-910311-52-8 $7.99

God's Rebels
by Henry Lee Curry III
From his unique perspective, Dr. Henry Lee Curry III offers a fascinating look at the lives of some of our greatest Southern religious leaders during the Civil War. The rampant Evangelical Christianity prominent at the outbreak of the Civil War, asserts Dr. Curry, is directly traceable to the 2nd Great Awakening of the early 1800s. The evangelical tradition, with its emphasis on strict morality, individual salvation, and emotional worship, had influenced most of Southern Protestantism by this time. Southerners unquestionably believed the voice of the ministers to be the "voice of God;" consequently, the church became one of the most powerful forces influencing Confederate life and morale. Inclined toward a Calvinistic emphasis on predestination, the South was confident that God would sustain its way of life.

ISBN: 0-910311-67-6 $12.99 Trade paper
ISBN: 0-910311-68-4 $21.99 Hardcover

Hidden Dangers of the Rainbow
by Constance Cumbey
The first book to uncover and expose the New Age movement, this national #1 best-seller paved the way for all other books on the subject. It has become a giant in its category. This book provides the vivid expose of the New Age movement, which the author contends is dedicated to wiping out Christianity and establishing a one world order. This movement, a vast network of occult and pagan organizations, meets the tests of prophecy concerning the Anti-christ.

ISBN 0-910311-03-X $9.99

Image of the Ages
by Dr. David Webber

Are the secular humanists' plans for the New World Order about to be realized? How will the establishment of this order affect you and your family? David Webber, author of *The Image of the Ages*, explains how modern technology, artificial intelligenece, and other scientific advances will be used in the near future to manipulate the masses.

ISBN 0-910311-38-2 $7.99

Kinsey, Sex and Fraud: The Indoctrination of a People
by Dr. Judith A. Reisman and Edward Eichel

Kinsey, Sex and Fraud describes the research of Alfred Kinsey which shaped Western society's beliefs and understanding of the nature of human sexuality. His unchallenged conclusions are taught at every level of education—elementary, high school and college—and quoted in textbooks as undisputed truth.

The authors clearly demonstrate that Kinsey's research involved illegal experimentations on several hundred children. The survey was carried out on a non-representative group of Americans, including disproportionately large numbers of sex offenders, prostitutes, prison inmates and exhibitionists.

ISBN 0-910311-20-X $19.95 Hard cover

Last Days Collection
by Last Days Ministries

Heart-stirring, faith challenging messages from Keith Green, David Wilkerson, Melody Green, Leonard Ravenhill, Winkie Pratney, Charles Finney, and William Booth are designed to awaken complacent Christians to action.

ISBN 0-961-30020-5 $8.99

Order These Huntington House Books !

_____	America Betrayed—Marlin Maddoux	$6.99 _____
_____	*Angel Vision (A Novel)—Jim Carroll with Jay Gaines	5.99 _____
_____	*Battle Plan: Equipping the Church for the 90s—Chris Stanton	7.99 _____
_____	Blessings of Liberty—Charles C. Heath	8.99 _____
_____	Cover of Darkness (A Novel)—J. Carroll	7.99 _____
_____	Crystalline Connection (A Novel)—Bob Maddux	8.99 _____
_____	Deadly Deception: Freemasonry—Tom McKenney	7.99 _____
_____	The Delicate Balance—John Zajac	8.99 _____
_____	Dinosaurs and the Bible—Dave Unfred	12.99 _____
_____	*Don't Touch That Dial—Barbara Hattemer & Robert Showers	9.99/19.99 _____
_____	En Route to Global Occupation—Gary Kah	9.99 _____
_____	Exposing the AIDS Scandal—Dr. Paul Cameron	7.99 _____
_____	*Face the Wind—Gloria Delaney	9.99 _____
_____	*False Security—Jerry Parks	9.99 _____
_____	From Rock to Rock—Eric Barger	8.99 _____
_____	Hidden Dangers of the Rainbow—Constance Cumbey	8.99 _____
_____	*Hitler and the New Age—Bob Rosio	9.99 _____
_____	The Image of the Ages—David Webber	7.99 _____
_____	Inside the New Age Nightmare—Randall Baer	8.99 _____
_____	*A Jewish Conservative Looks at Pagan America—Don Feder	9.99/19.99 _____
_____	*Journey Into Darkness—Stephen Arrington	9.99 _____
_____	Kinsey, Sex and Fraud—Dr. Judith A. Reisman &	19.99 _____
	Edward Eichel (Hard cover)	8.99 _____
_____	Last Days Collection—Last Days Ministries	8.95 _____
_____	Legend of the Holy Lance (A Novel)—William T. Still	
	(Paper/Hard cover)	8.99/16.99 _____
_____	New World Order—William T. Still	9.99 _____
_____	*One Year to a College Degree—Lynette Long & Eileen	9.99 _____
	Hershberger	
_____	*Political Correctness—David Thibodaux (Paper/Hard cover)	9.99/18.99 _____
_____	Psychic Phenomena Unveiled—John Anderson	8.99 _____
_____	Seduction of the Innocent Revisited—John Fulce	8.99 _____
_____	"Soft Porn" Plays Hardball—Dr. Judith A. Reisman	
	(Paper/Hard cover)	8.99/16.99 _____
_____	*Subtle Serpent—Darylann Whitemarsh & Bill Reisman	9.99 _____
_____	Teens and Devil-Worship—Charles G.B. Evans	8.99 _____
_____	To Grow By Storybook Readers—Janet Friend	44.95 per set _____
_____	Touching the Face of God—Bob Russell (Paper/Hardcover)	8.99/18.99 _____
_____	Twisted Cross—Joseph Carr	9.99 _____
_____	*When the Wicked Seize a City—Chuck & Donna McIlhenny with	9.99 _____
	Frank York	
_____	Who Will Rule the Future?—Paul McGuire	8.99 _____
_____	*You Hit Like a Girl—Elsa Houtz & William J. Ferkile	9.99 _____
	Shipping and Handling	_____

* New Titles

TOTAL _____

AVAILABLE AT BOOKSTORES EVERYWHERE or order direct from: _____

Huntington House Publishers • P.O. Box 53788 • Lafayette, LA 70505
Send check/money order. For faster service use VISA/MASTERCARD

call toll-free 1-800-749-4009.

Add: Freight and handling, $3.50 for the first book ordered, and $.50 for each additional book up to 5 books.

Enclosed is $ _____ including postage.

VISA/MASTERCARD# _____ Exp. Date _____

Name _____

Address _____

City, State, Zip code _____